DECISION AND INFLUENCE PROCESSES IN PRIVATE PENSION PLANS

Pension Research Council

PENSION RESEARCH COUNCIL PUBLICATIONS

Decision and Influence Processes
in Private Pension Plans

by
JAMES E. McNULTY, Jr.

Associate Professor of Industry
Wharton School of Finance and Commerce
University of Pennsylvania

Published for the

Pension Research Council
Wharton School of Finance and Commerce
University of Pennsylvania

by

RICHARD D. IRWIN, INC.
Homewood, Illinois

PURPOSE OF THE COUNCIL

The Pension Research Council of the Wharton School of Finance and Commerce was created in 1952 for the purpose of sponsoring objective research in the area of private pensions. It was formed in response to the urgent need for a better understanding of the private pension movement. Private pensions have experienced a phenomenal growth during the last two decades, but their economic, political, and social implications are yet to be explored. They seem destined to play a major role in the quest for old-age economic security, but the nature of that role can be ascertained only on the basis of a more enlightened evaluation of the capabilities and limitations of the private pension mechanism. It was to conduct an impartial study into the facts and basic issues surrounding private pensions, under the auspices of an academic and professional group representing leadership in every phase of the field, that the Council was organized.

Projects undertaken by the Council are broad in scope and predominantly interpretive rather than technical in nature. In general, attention is concentrated on areas which are not the object of special investigation by other research groups. Its research studies are conducted by mature scholars drawn from both the academic and business spheres. Research results are published from time to time in a series of books and monographs.

MEMBERS OF TASK FORCE IV

JAMES E. McNULTY, Jr., *Chairman,* Associate Professor of Industry, Wharton School of Finance and Commerce, Philadelphia

DAVIS W. GREGG, *President,* American College of Life Underwriters, Bryn Mawr, Pa.

KENNETH C. FOSTER, *Vice President,* The Prudential Insurance Company of America, Newark

SAMUEL A. MILLER, *Actuary,* Pension Plan Consulting Service, Washington, D.C.

JOHN B. ST. JOHN, *Consulting Actuary,* Penllyn, Pa.

CARL STEVENSON, *Assistant Treasurer,* Eastman Kodak Company, Rochester

LAZARE TEPER, *Research Director,* International Ladies Garment Workers Union, New York City

FOREWORD

This volume is the third publication to emerge from the Pension Research Council's inquiry into the factual basis of benefit expectations under private pension plans. The first volume, *Legal Protection of Private Pension Expectations,* by Professor Edwin W. Patterson, presented the results of a comprehensive survey of the legal rules, principles, and procedures—common law and statutory, judicial and administrative—presently available in the United States for the protection of employee benefit expectations. The second publication, *Legal Status of Employee Benefit Rights under Private Pension Plans,* by Professor Benjamin Aaron, dealt with a related but more narrow topic. Professor Aaron's research was directed at the legal bases of employee rights under private pension plans and the impact on those rights of various acts of the employer, the employee, or the bargaining representative of the employees.

This volume, based on a field study of firms and unions maintaining pension plans and agencies servicing those plans, presents an integrated treatment of the administrative and operational phases of pension activity in the United States, with the objective of assessing the likely impact of these forces on the security of pension benefits. Professor McNulty, a student of administrative organization and decision making, has examined with penetrating insight the pension operations of industrial firms, unions, banks, insurance companies, mutual funds, actuaries, accountants, independent administrators, investment counselors, and lawyers. The result is a multidimensional picture of the institutional framework of the

ix

American private pension system, focused on the theme of pension security.

In his undertaking, Professor McNulty had access to the counsel and guidance of a specially constituted group of pension experts, identified as Task Force IV. The project director wishes to express his deep appreciation to the members of Task Force IV for their generous and effective contribution to this phase of the over-all inquiry. Thanks are also due to the Pension Research Council and many other individuals who responded to Professor McNulty's requests for information and consultation. Finally, the project director records his gratitude to Professor McNulty for undertaking this assignment and carrying it out with such enthusiasm, insight, and thoroughness.

DAN M. MCGILL
Project Director

Philadelphia
October 1961

PREFACE

The approach used in this study of American private pension plans will probably strike many readers as something of a departure from existing pension literature. The emphasis was not on detailed description, for its own sake, of pension plans and the institutions supporting them. Nor was there any intent of showing the relative merits of any particular type of pension plan—public or private.

The object instead was the simple one of attempting to characterize the decision and influence processes associated with prevailing pension arrangements in the United States. The typical operating pension plan is really a collection of many subprograms and procedures, some of them worked out within the sponsoring organization, others by the various agencies which service the plan. As is well known to students of administration, these parts of a good system (1) must be produced through adequate planning, (2) should be compatible with each other, and (3) should reflect in their concept and operation the underlying objectives—presumably adequate and secure pensions—rather than various ancillary considerations which might be in the minds of decision-makers and operators. An investigation of such considerations as these is the concern here.

Most of the attention in the study is directed to the single-employer type of plan, both conventional and negotiated. Single-employer plans are more numerous, of course, than multiple-employer plans at the present time. Also, being individual and being relatively free from requirements for conformity to a pattern of operation, they are a good deal more

xi

varied with respect to their operating features. This is not to say that multiple-employer plans are so standard as not to be worth talking about; to the contrary, a chapter has been devoted to them.

In the discussion of pension funding and service agencies it will be quite obvious that the apportionment of space does not reflect the present relative importance of the several agencies in handling pension functions. The reason for this variance is the concern of this part of the study with the identifiable agency arrangements in the pension field rather than with a simple profile. The general rule followed has been to give space to all agency activities in the pension field which are not obviously freakish or *ad hoc*.

Monographs such as the present one are certainly the product of the particular interest of the writer. But they also reflect the help and cooperation of a great many other people. Much of whatever value the present study may possess is attributable to the assistance of the members of Task Force IV of the Study of the Security of Pension Benefits, to the many representatives of employers, unions, and pension agencies who were interviewed, to the members of the Pension Research Council, and to Professor Dan McGill, who has been at once colleague, tutor, and friend. I am very grateful for all the help I received from these people and, of course, exonerate them for any shortcomings of this work.

Mrs. Helen White expertly typed the manuscript in its various stages. Miss Mildred Brill of the S. S. Huebner Foundation was most helpful and patient in expediting the procedural requirements germane to the conduct of the study.

J. E. M.

October, 1961

TABLE OF CONTENTS

xiii

Chapter I

INTRODUCTION

Purpose and General Scope

The present report and the field investigation which underlies it attempt to throw light on the administrative and working phases, as distinguished from actuarial and legal aspects, of pension activity in the United States. In the first instance we look in on the managerial procedures and arrangements developed by sponsoring employers for their pension plans, as well as those arrangements that have come into existence in the case of multiple-employer collectively bargained plans. We then turn our attention to the funding agencies—banks, insurance companies, and mutual funds— and to the service agencies—actuaries, consultants, independent administrators, investment counselors, public accountants, and lawyers—which taken together might be described as the American pension "industry." Finally we try to put together the facts and analysis of plan administration and supporting institutions with the view of commenting on their implications for the security of pension benefits.

There are indeed many factors directly affecting the security of pension benefits. The guarantees offered under private pension arrangements, the substantive financial provisions for meeting pension promises, the granting of proprietary rights to pensions through early vesting, the legal

1

status of private pensions, and the stability of the dollar all have an important bearing on the fulfillment of pension expectations. By concentrating on the administrative and working phases of private pension activity we certainly do not mean to imply that what is done in these other areas is of limited or no importance.[1]

On the other hand, it seems quite clear that the most laudable policies which might be developed by employers, unions, funding and service agencies, and regulatory bodies for the purpose of making pension benefits secure are of dubious value if such policies have not been developed with an eye to the institutional "facts of life" germane to pension processes. Policies of any kind must be implemented, and, if this is not possible or has not been effectively provided for, the policies tend to become meaningless.

Also policies, whether public or private, governing the operation of one facet of a process or system must be reconcilable and reconciled with policies developed for other facets if there are not to be internal contradictions. This latter point seems particularly important in the case of private pension plans because, being privately sponsored and operated, their administration is decentralized in our economy. Any treatment of them which abstracts from these circumstances and their implications, favorable and unfavorable, for the security of pension benefits will quite obviously be seriously incomplete.

For these reasons, as well as because of the intrinsic

---

[1] Other Task Forces of the Pension Research Council have or will report on these other areas. See Edwin W. Patterson, *Legal Protection of Private Pension Expectations* (Homewood, Ill.; Richard D. Irwin, Inc., 1960) ; Benjamin Aaron, *Legal Status of Employee Benefit Rights under Private Pension Plans* (Homewood, Ill.: Richard D. Irwin, Inc., 1961) ; Carl Fischer and William Marples, *Actuarial Aspects of Pension Security* (Homewood, Ill.: Richard D. Irwin, Inc., forthcoming) ; Dan M. McGill, *Fulfilling Pension Expectations* (Homewood, Ill.: Richard D. Irwin, Inc., forthcoming).

interest of the subject, the present study is focused upon the separate, but connected, processes which have become germane to the private pension movement in the United States. The relevant standard for the success of this type of inquiry is the extent to which it gets inside of and behind available data on the broad characteristics of the private pension structure. What we want to know are three things: (1) the patterns of variation underlying these broad characteristics; (2) the reasons for these variations; and (3) the interactions and the influence of the various parts and people of the pension structure upon each other and upon the whole. As has been suggested these data are certainly essential if one wants to talk intelligently about the subject of pension security, even though other considerations, notably actuarial and legal, enter in also.

Previous Work on the Subject

By and large the written record pertinent to the subject of administrative and working phases of private pension activity is fragmentary and scattered. There have been some studies, however, which have dealt in a larger way with these phases than has been customary. The Mooney Report on the New York State Banking Department survey of funds held by state and national banks presents, among other things, data on surface organizational and authority relationships for several hundred pension plans trusteed by New York state banks, as well as certain data concerned with working relationships existing between employers and trustees, on the one hand, and banks and actuaries on the other.[2] It is suggested by these data that there are great differences in the handling of private pension plans.

---

[2] George A. Mooney, *Pension and Other Employee Welfare Plans*, Preliminary Report (New York State, 1955).

The House Report for the New York State Insurance Department draws something of a profile of the private employee benefit field for the purpose of discussing its regulation.[3] In so doing the report touches upon a number of subjects of interest, including especially the position of corporate trustees vis à vis the sponsors of pension plans, the choices to be made by actuaries in estimating the financial requirements of plans, and the position of insurance agents and brokers. At various points also there is speculation concerning the nature of the influence processes operating in the pension field in general and on those operators just enumerated in particular. The general burden of this speculation is that there are a number of undesirable influences from the standpoint of the security and size of employee benefits, including pensions.

Very recently a study of the private pension field by Harbrecht for the Twentieth Century Fund explores similar territory.[4] Among the points made in this study of interest in the present context are that company pension boards, frequently used especially for the administration of pension benefits, are likely to be beholden to a cost-conscious management and that bank trustees and other service agencies may be in a similar position as the result of the nature of their vendor relationship.

Useful and provocative as these studies are, they quite obviously stop short of fulfilling the need outlined in the preceding section. In the first place, data showing differences in internal administration of pension plans and working relationships with funding and service agencies do not make clear what these differences signify.

---

[3] State of New York, Insurance Department, *Private Employee Benefit Plans—a Public Trust*, submitted by Martin S. House, Special Counsel (1956).

[4] Paul P. Harbrecht, S.J., *Pension Funds and Economic Power* (New York: Twentieth Century Fund, 1959), especially chap. 4.

Another point is that speculation on influence processes within and among firms and individuals is not enough when it is based simply upon gross authority relationships or broad legal relationships. It is a commonplace of the modern analysis of competition, for example, that a contract is only one means of establishing the market position of a vendor with a buyer. Despite the frequent weakness of the language from the vendor's point of view there are other devices, some persuasive, some tied up with the broader characteristics of industrial competition, which serve to equalize power positions between vendor and buyer and which thereby give the vendor some "say" about what crosses the market place and at what terms.[5]

Modern research in the field of business organization and control suggests the same thing about internal authority relationships in business. For one thing a subordinate may be given considerable discretion in carrying on his work. Much more important here has been the discovery that administrative control systems used in business are often not effective enough to insure the carrying out of top management's wishes.[6] This fact constitutes something of a double-edged sword as far as pension security is concerned. For example, a company pension administrator, recognizing that he was being judged in terms of cost performance, might within his area of discretion be less liberal in his treatment of employees and pensioners than top management really wanted him to be. Fortunately, the nature of control and reporting procedures used for company pension boards and individual administrators in most cases seems not to pro-

---

[5] The literature here is diffuse. However, some detail can be gotten from J. S. Bain's book, *Barriers to New Competition* (Cambridge, Mass.: Harvard University Press, 1956), especially chap. ii.

[6] Cf. J. G. March and H. A. Simon, *Organizations* (New York: John Wiley & Sons, Inc., 1958), chaps. 2–3.

vide much incentive for such behavior on the part of pension administrators.[7]

Methodology Used in the Present Study

In view of the objectives of the present study and the problems which seem to pervade previous studies in the same area the investigative technique used here has necessarily been rather different, although not unorthodox for purposes of the sort which have been described. The main vehicle aside from the written record has been the field interview. Influential persons in forty-eight firms with pension plans, funding institutions, and service agencies were interviewed, usually at considerable length. From these forty-eight interviews information was obtained not only about the firms and agencies interviewed and their operations but also about the operations and policies of an even greater number of other pension plans and agencies with whom the interviewees were linked collaboratively or competitively. The effective coverage of the study is hence somewhat greater than first meets the eye, although it is clear that the part of information which was gained indirectly has to be interpreted with special care.

The firms whose pension plans were investigated directly by these methods tended, by and large, to be concentrated in the manufacturing field. Their size, measured in terms of covered employees, was distributed more or less evenly, however. In the case of those plans which were studied directly the range was from as few as sixty-five employees to the tens of thousands covered in the pension plans of the industrial giants.

The funding agencies talked to included old and recent large operators in the pension field, as well as smaller but

---

[7] See Chapter III.

very aggressive agencies outside of the New York City area. Included in the service agencies talked to were actuarial, administrative, and investment specialists, as well as firms offering multiple services to pension clients.

The field interviews were conducted solely by the writer, rather than by a staff of assistants. This procedure necessarily cut down the number of cases which could be examined directly or indirectly and put a much greater weight on the judgmental faculties of the writer and his Task Force advisors as far as the representativeness of the sample is concerned. As is clear from the writer's questionnaire guides and record forms, shown in the Appendix, the procedure was almost necessary because of the "soft" nature of the data being obtained and the consequent problems of interpretation and comparison. It is possible that a larger sample would have suggested radically different results concerning the nature of pension processes. However, the writer's experience as an administrative and institutional analyst suggests that this is not probable. The validity of this position it is hoped will become apparent in the discussion of pension administration and working relationships which we shall now undertake.

Chapter II

DEVELOPMENT OF PENSION PLANS
BY INDIVIDUAL EMPLOYERS

Genesis of the Idea

Two interesting points emerged from inquiring into the beginnings of pension plans. One is that, generally speaking, top management, including especially the boards of directors in larger companies, is extremely active at this stage of the process. A perusal of the sales management literature put out, for example, by the insurance companies for their agents suggests that this fact is well understood in what we have called the "pension industry."

The second point emerging from this phase of the study is perhaps less well understood. It is that, moving over the years into the present time, the role of top management, while still of primary importance in the introduction of a pension plan in a company, seems less and less to include the crucial element of initiation of the idea. Increasingly the initial influence, if it comes from within the company at all, comes from below, very often from the company personnel officer, occasionally from the treasurer's department.

There are a number of possible reasons for this change. One undoubtedly is the number of sales and development people operating for the several funding and service agencies. Not only is this larger number of sales personnel likely

8

to have explored the different ways of making headway with a prospect company, but also as a group they probably have the effect of making pension programs a less unusual field of management action than they formerly were.[1] It was usually the case in talking with companies whose pension programs were started well before World War II to hear that the originator was the president or chief executive officer whose interest was not especially a desire to increase his competitive position in the labor markets but rather a more idealistic motive such as, for example, insuring that his retired employees would be able to live in relative financial independence and with dignity.

A more important reason for the change observed in the locus of initiation of pension plans in companies is probably the recognition by company personnel people that, especially since the Great Depression, old-age security has become a significant desire in the preferences of employees. With this, pensions have become a relevant dimension and tool of company competitiveness in labor markets. As an instrument of operation of an important function of a business, it would be almost queer in terms of what is known about the theory and practice of management for initiation of pension activity not to come from below in a firm of any reasonable size.[2]

Finally, the change of initiation locus in pension plans has without doubt been influenced by events at the collective bargaining table. Knowing something of the interests of their rank and file and armed by the Inland Steel Decision

---

[1] Cf. Dan M. McGill, *Fundamentals of Private Pensions* (Homewood, Ill.: Richard D. Irwin, Inc., 1955), pp. 13 ff.

[2] For empirical evidence of this point see Robert A. Gordon, *Business Leadership in the Large Corporation* (Washington, D.C. Brookings Institution, 1945), chaps. 3–4. For a relevant argument see Peter Drucker, *The Practice of Management* (New York: Harper & Bros., Inc., 1954), chap. 17.

of 1949, which legitimatized pensions as a subject for collective bargaining, union negotiators confronted company negotiators with the subject of pensions. While the interviews of the present study suggested that in a number of instances company negotiators privately have been somewhat ahead of union leaders in thinking of various kinds of pension enhancement, including such things as vesting, and have held back only for tactical reasons, it would be unreasonable to neglect the importance of unions as a force in the initiation of pensions. This point seems a reasonable inference to be drawn from the starting dates, as well as the stated circumstances surrounding many of the plans which were encountered in the present study.

Structural Decisions

It appears to be almost universally true with single-employer plans that the company president or, if it is active, the board of directors of a company makes the decisions which determine the basic structure of a pension plan, including coverage, benefit formula, contribution system, and funding method (although in the case of negotiated pension plans all these decisions are often not made unilaterally).

It appeared to be true that the president and board approach these structural questions with a great deal of thought and study when a pension program is being started in a company. This seems a very reasonable state of affairs in consideration of the usually substantial financial implications of a pension plan, as well as the size and substance of the moral, if not legal, obligations entailed.

However a point frequently made in this connection by the company personnel interviewed was that when a plan was being initially structured top management or the board tended to rely almost exclusively on outside advice notably from actuarial consultants and representatives of funding media who had been invited to consult. While the specialized nature of such things as benefit formula development was conceded, two criticisms were common. One was that the board took too much time developing the plan and that important personnel and financial advantages were thereby lost. Another and potentially more serious criticism from the standpoint of pension security was that on occasion the outside consultants used by the board did not or were not in a position to take the fullest advantage of relevant information available within the company.

A case cited in point by a company executive interviewed was the failure of the consulting actuary to make the correct wage progression assumption in the case of a plan with a final average salary provision in its benefit formula. Apparently the fault was not so much that of the actuary as it was of a board member who for one reason or another —possibly deliberately—insisted that the actuary reduce substantially his original estimate. In any case the effect eventually was to make the company's annual contribution substantially greater than had been planned and to cause at least a temporary cessation in the amortization of past service liability.

Conceivably these criticisms of board decision-making procedure at the outset of a pension plan are generated more often by emotion or lack of information than by substance. On the other hand, a communications gap between the outside consultants and those people within a company who have immediate access to important data is conceivable at the outset of a plan, given the observed method of decision-making and given the diverse interests which sometimes operate within a firm. As the case cited shows, this sort of communications gap can lead to rather serious consequences.

Hence it would seem advisable that all parties in this stage of the decision process—the various elements of top management and the outside advisors—should take care that they are not relying on the faulty information which will be provided by a defective company control system.

Other Decision Areas

In the single-employer plans which are being discussed in this chapter, decisions on such matters as what constitutes continuity of service for purposes of pension payment, relevant compensation levels if the plan has a selective salary average provision in its benefit formula, and what constitutes total and permanent disability if the plan has such a feature, are characteristically left to company pension boards or individual administrators, except in the case of some negotiated plans where pertinent definitions and procedures are spelled out in great detail. It appears to be true, however, that at the beginning of the operation of a pension plan when policies and procedures on the matters enumerated are being worked out for the first time, top-management interest is maintained and approvals by it required. Subsequently top-level control tends to rest on examination of an annual report to the company board of directors from the company pension board or administrator. An important exception occurs in the case of some small companies in which the president remains close to the situation and some large companies which operate on the "exception" principle of management, that is to say, which require nonroutine questions to be referred upward in the organization.

It seems quite obvious that sufficient direction is given at the ouset to pension boards and administrators who have these responsibilities relating to eligibility, relevant compensation levels, and disability. Whether or not this constitutes sufficient direction ultimately depends very much upon the degree of anticipation of future conditions exercised early in the plan, given the usual ultimate control system. Also, as has been suggested in the opening chapter of this book, there is always the question of what is the true basis of action of an administrator unless he is controlled by his superiors in terms of all the details of his operation. Obviously this latter point is likely to be less of a question from a pensioner standpoint when there is a company pension *board* and especially when it has employee as well as management representatives on it. The problem also disappears to the extent that top management is committed to an enlightened personnel policy and is informationally, in terms of knowing what goes on in the minds of its employees, in a position to enforce such a policy on middle management. As it turned out, there were actually no indications of abuse of authority by pension boards or by administrators in the case of the companies investigated in the present study. More will be said about the subject in Chapter III.

Plan Amendments

While top management retains and exercises its approval function as regards amendments to and changes in the structure and mode of operation of pension plans, the pressure for such changes seems almost always to come from below. Either those executives charged with operating the plan or operating with it, or, in the case of the very large firm with abundant staff resources, the specialists charged with studying pension developments are typically the initiators of change.

This point seems certainly to hold in the matter of liberalizations in benefits, vesting privileges, and the like. Company personnel officers have an interest in these things.

Also, as has been suggested above, the company negotiators often encounter pressure for liberalization from their union counterparts who presumably are in the business of establishing more liberal wage and fringe patterns.

The writer was told by many representatives of funding agencies that changes in funding agency and method are most frequently the result of pressures applied directly to the board of directors of a company by representatives of funding agencies who happen to sit on the board or who take advantage of a friendly business or social connection with board members. While it would be foolish to deny the existence of such lines of influence, the writer's observation was that most typically the company treasurer or chief financial officer (possibly as the result of influence exerted from the outside) was the key actor. This seemed to be true in both larger and smaller firms.

While no instances were uncovered of company treasurers openly disagreeing with their respective boards of directors on the question of the best funding arrangement, this primary role of company treasurers seems reasonable for at least two reasons. The first is that the company treasurer by virtue of his training and his responsibilities is usually watching, if not working on, the financial management of his company's pension program. Unless he is very fixed in his ideas about funding arrangements—and occasionally such a person was encountered in the interviews— he is likely to be looking for ways which he thinks will better his company's over-all financial position and is therefore very susceptible to new information from any source. These points will receive further attention in Chapter IV.

The second reason for accepting the observed importance of company financial people in basic financial changes in pension plans is simply that a company's board, while it may include a person or persons very favorable to particular funding arrangements, is likely to include other persons of different disposition. If the director favorable to a particular financial agency or method does not have the company's operating financial people "in his corner," so to speak, explanations may well be required. Further, even when a particular group prevails in a matter of this sort, results must be forthcoming. In this vein one case was turned up in the field interviews in which an important company president made a controversial change in the locus of financial management authority for his company's pension plan. The results were disappointing, and, while no stockholder suits were reported, the president's reputation as a judicious executive had quite clearly been severely damaged.

On the other side of the ledger on this question of company treasurer influence on financial changes in plans it must be said it was quite clear that in the case of very large companies, boards of directors were by no means under the domination of their operating financial people. Presumably this is to be explained in part by the caliber and backgrounds of board members of such companies. Also in many of these instances the board had directed that special studies be made by the company's pertinent professional staff as an alternative both to outside sales pressure and also to advice normally furnished by the operating financial officers.

Mergers and Management Decentralization

Special problems for the firm which acquires other firms or for the firm whose policy it is to maintain a strong degree of local managerial autonomy are suggested by the preceding discussion with its emphasis on the influence of operating financial management on pension plans. A prediction in the case of the firm with a policy of local managerial autonomy is, of course, relatively easy once pensions have been established as essentially a financial matter or function in the firm (and this apparently is the trend, as will be suggested in Chapter IV). Centralization of financial management is the almost uniform exception to local autonomy policies.[3]

It was found in the course of the field work that some multilocation companies were still trying to practice substantial decentralization of management in connection with pension activity. The theory was that pensions were essentially personnel matters which should be within the purview of local plant management. Such attempts, however, were usually beset with problems arising from nonuniformity, which often provides a negotiation wedge for unions. Also there were problems arising essentially from the lack of adequate specialized advice to local management. It seems unlikely that such experiments in actual decentralization will be maintained.

This is not to say that the *appearance* of decentralization in pension management will not be maintained, since this apparently has collective bargaining advantages from a management point of view. One of the interesting things which appeared at first glance in the study of multilocation firms was the apparent split in philosophy of management, with one group being quite frank in saying that pension matters for the company were run out of the home office and with the other emphasizing the discretionary authority of plant managers. Further investigation revealed, however, that plant managers of multilocation firms, while they might have nominal and official discretion in pension matters, seldom exercised such discretion without contacting the ap-

---

[3] Cf. Gordon, *op. cit.*

propriate home office official or staffer with responsibility for pension affairs, and furthermore were expected not to proceed on their own except in the most extraordinary and unbelievable circumstances.

The typical procedure in the case of the multilocation firm is for a master pension policy or plan to be developed at the home office.[4] This plan is then imposed *in toto* or else used as the frame of reference for any pension negotiations which take place at the local level.[5] When in the case of locally negotiated plans many unions are involved, management usually attempts to negotiate essentially the same plan with each union. The companies interviewed who follow this procedure apparently have done so with a considerable degree of success. One reason probably has been the relative liberality of the plans offered by these particular companies in comparison with the patterns demanded by the unions involved. In many cases the latter have their own strategy

---

[4] In a number of cases it was observed that there were actually two or three separate master plans, one for salaried workers, (and) executives, and one for hourly workers reflecting differences in interests in these groups. While the separate plans were not discriminatory, sometimes the funding arrangements were different—for example, an insurance company for the salaried plan and a bank trustee for the hourly. A more important exception to the rule stated in the text arises in the case of American companies with substantial operations overseas. Here the policy is to develop separate plans for foreign nationals employed by the company. Such plans are tailored to the needs, customs, and patterns of the particular country. In some places, such as parts of Latin America, private pensions have a limited role because of the existence of social security systems with relatively high benefits.

[5] In many cases it is virtually necessary to have separate plans because of different unions. However, from a management point of view there are apparently some advantages to separation especially of the funding arrangement in a multilocation firm. Where they have been permitted to do so by the collective bargaining situation some companies have set up technically separate plans at different locations. The reason was quite frankly stated to be a hedge against having to shut down a plant. If such a plant were to have a high proportion of retired or eligible-to-retire workers the drain from partial termination, given termination provisions favoring these groups, would be substantial. If there were an integrated fund this drain would hence tend to force up the schedule of contributions for that part of the plan retained.

worked out centrally and tailored to the average pension-paying abilities of the employers organized by them. It is of interest here that in a number of cases an international union with its own multiple-employer plan has allowed companies to substitute their own, more liberal plans, although the reverse certainly has happened too.

Another reason for the success of the master policy approach in negotiations with several unions apparently has been the tendency to parallelism in the demands of many of the larger unions. Part of this is undoubtedly due to the similarities which at times characterize union wage demands in our present-day economy. Partly the parallelism may be attributable to informal consultation on pension matters which apparently goes on among some of our bigger unions.

In the case of a merger between two companies or the acquisition of one by the other the common practice seems to be to close out one or both of the premerger plans in favor of a postmerger plan if the two companies are to be fully integrated with each other. This may be done immediately or over a period of time by not allowing new entrants. Such a course is obviously reasonable from the standpoint of personnel policy, especially since intracompany transfer of employees is thereby facilitated. Whether or not one of the premerger plans is retained as the common postmerger plan presumably depends upon the attitude of top management towards the two premerger plans.[6]

When the acquired company is allowed to operate as an affiliate or subsidiary the postpurchase practice fre-

---

[6] Presumably also the thinking on this problem and the implications of substituting a new plan is done as part of the analysis connected with a merger or acquisition. However, it was indicated in some of the field interviews that the question of what to do about pensions had been overlooked until after the advent of the merger or acquisition. This certainly has a pension security aspect although outright discontinuances of pension plans with no alternative being offered to employees probably are not common in merger circumstances today.

quently is somewhat different in that the affiliate may be allowed to retain its existing plan. Such a course seems reasonable also. For one thing affiliates and subsidiaries are probably often in different industry fields than the parent company, and there may be differences in pension pattern. Also in the case of the acquiring of a technical affiliate, which is quite common these days, the suggestion of local autonomy given by retention of an existing pension plan quite clearly can be beneficial from a personnel point of view.[7]

Nevertheless, in line with what has been said above the practice of centralizing financial decisions in the firm, it is definitely not the practice to allow an affiliate or subsidiary to make changes in its pension plan without guidance from responsible officials and/or specialists of the parent corporation. Furthermore it appears to be generally the practice on the part of the parent corporation to encourage changes which will make the affiliate plans more like those of the parent company in such basic matters as benefit levels and formulae, contribution system, and coverage. The use of local actuarial and other consultants is often continued. However, it is frequently the practice to subordinate these groups in policy matters to the consultants to the parent company.

Evaluation

If one were to attempt to evaluate these facts concerning the development of pension plans by employers, one would generally approve of the sense of responsibility seemingly shown by top management and boards of directors

---

[7] Cf. Samuel E. Hill and Frederick Harbison, *Manpower and Innovation in American Industry*, Princeton University Industrial Relations Section, Research Report # 96 (1959), for a discussion of problems of technical personnel.

in overseeing the structuring and restructuring of these plans. Such activity is certainly suggestive of a sense of obligation felt by these groups for making good on the promises implicit in the pension arrangements made. The fact that these groups are increasingly less active in the initiation of plans and changes in plans is probably more indicative of improved methods of business administration than of less interest, since the functions of boards of directors and top management are usually deemed to be more of an overseeing than an operating nature.

The possible communications gap, noted previously, between consultants to the board in the initial structuring of plans and internal sources of relevant information is of some concern, especially since it is entirely plausible. The effect of such a gap is to lower the value of pension promises made in good faith by company managements. There are a number of forces in existence which are likely to prevent the discontinuance of a pension plan in circumstances less than bankruptcy for the sponsoring firm. However, pension costs are not an insignificant factor in the total financial picture of a firm. As such they are likely to be pared if it is possible when they are for any reason out of line and the circumstances of the firm require cost reduction.

Another point which will be of concern to some interested in pension security will be the pratice, noted in the discussion of pension management in multilocation firms, of technically separating the plans offered at different locations. Quite obviously such a practice endangers the pensions of those located at potentially uneconomical sites, unless of course each plan has sufficient funds.

This problem is a difficult one to evaluate. On the one hand, a deliberate hedge by management with respect to its pension promises is hard to condone. But on the other hand, the possibility of being able to make such a hedge is probably a factor, if not making possible the introduction of a pension plan, certainly in the level of benefits and other conditions of a plan. We shall return to this problem as it affects pensioners and near pensioners in the concluding chapter of this book and say now only that some measures other than the obvious alternative of prohibiting such a hedge as a condition for qualification of a pension plan might be considered.

Chapter III

OPERATION OF SINGLE-EMPLOYER PLANS: PENSION ADMINISTRATION BY EMPLOYERS

Areas of Operating Responsibility

All pension plans, once they have been started either as policies or programs, entail certain working activities, including especially financial planning and action, record-keeping, communication, and the dispensing of benefits. Before employers began to follow the practice of having formal pension plans, these activities were all probably carried on as part of the normal activities of the company, although undoubtedly on more of an *ad hoc* basis than would be considered proper today. In one utility studied which until recently had an informal pension plan it appeared to be true that the only special operation connected with the pension plan was the occasional granting of pensions to employees retiring. In this particular instance it was the practice for the board to vote the pension upon recommendation of the company personnel officer.

With the growth of formal pension plans, the initial impact seems to have been that most if not all of the working activities just enumerated typically were put into the hands of an outside agency, usually an insurance company. When bank-trusteed plans became common, investment and pension administration was put into the hands of banks and the pension service agencies, including especially the consultants and actuaries. Together these agencies handled the work which needed to be done in the implementation of the pension plan.

While many of these "subcontracting" arrangements have been maintained, as the later chapters on funding and service agencies will spell out in detail, there has been considerable reintegration of pension functions into the present-day operations of employers. This fact is responsible for this chapter, on pension administration by employers, and the chapter following on financial management activities.

The degree of integration is not likely to be a constant, as the present development of mutual fund activity in the pension field suggests,[1] but it seems quite likely that many of the financial and administrative activities which have been taken over by employers will continue to be handled by them because of the close connection of some of these activities with the broadest problems of operating a business in an age of tight money, rising labor costs, and delicate labor relations.

Administration of Records

In the case of medium- and larger-sized companies nowadays, records of employees' service and wages for benefit administration, actuarial calculation, and other purposes are almost uniformly maintained in the company. This is quite natural and probably very economical in view of the need for such companies to keep systematic personnel records. There is probably some connection between the

---

[1] The usage of the word "integration" here and later is not to be confused with the usage which refers to pension formulas adjusted for social security benefits anticipated.

latter fact and the apparent decline of the insurance company as the record keeper and/or record-systems supervisor in the case of insured plans, including conventional group annuity plans as well as deposit administration plans. Under both of these arrangements the largest companies are likely to set up and maintain their own records, with a duplicate set always being kept by the insurance company only in the case of group annuity plans. The same development of record keeping in the largest firms has taken place in the case of bank-trusteed plans, although banks and pension consulting agencies probably were never as deeply involved in this operation for large firms as were formerly the insurance companies.

Ordinarily the records are kept in and under the initial jurisdiction of the personnel department, occasionally the controller. When a pension case arises the wage and service records are used for a pension calculation by the personnel people or by some group in the company treasurer's or financial department. The pension recommendation then goes to the pension administrator or board. In many cases the calculated pensions are checked by the consulting actuary to the company. If this is not done the actuary oversees the calculation procedures. The actuary uses the records also for calculating actuarial liability of a plan periodically.

For the largest firms there are two variations to the work flow just described which are important. The first is that when the pensions are granted by an administrative board which includes union representatives, a duplicate set of records may be kept by this group. The second is that in multiplant firms record keeping is sometimes decentralized to the personnel sections of the individual plants. The latter practice usually is found when pensions are initiated at the plant level and is therefore quite reasonable. Neither decentralization of record keeping nor decentralization of pension decisions is ever complete. Procedures for record keeping are worked out in the central office. As will be explained later in this section the initiation of pensions at the local level is done according to a uniform set of procedures worked out at the home office, possibly in connection with collective bargaining, and the results are controlled by a central agency.

Smaller and medium-sized firms are more likely to have an outside agency—an insurance company, bank, pension consultant, or actuary—to maintain records, or at least set up record-keeping procedures within the company, and to do the necessary pension calculations. The reason for this apparently is the difficulty many smaller and medium-sized companies have in maintaining records by themselves.

Also economics probably plays a part. Good data on costs of pension administration are difficult to obtain, as are administrative cost data in general, and were considered beyond the scope of this study. Nevertheless, in a number of instances where records were maintained within small and medium-sized firms, the writer observed what appeared to be high-cost hand operations which probably could be done more cheaply by a service organization using modern data-processing equipment.

Control of Record Keeping

Procedures for insuring that service and wage records of covered employees are correct and complete are varied and on the whole appear to be somewhat haphazard. One company which was interviewed relatively early in the field survey stated that it had its outside auditors do a complete enumeration each year of the covered employees in its plan whose benefits were based on service. This turned out to be a unique procedure as far as the whole group of companies studied was concerned and was generally regarded as carrying things too far. A number of companies apparently conduct an internal audit of procedures used in record keeping. However, this number is probably not a majority, one would judge from the companies studied as well as from talking with public accountants.[2]

As was suggested, insurance companies appear no longer to be invited or to insist on an internal audit of record keeping by their clients. Under some of the newer arrangements in which insurance companies participate, moreover, they apparently may waive the right to do so. It is true nevertheless that many insurance companies as well as banks do attempt to make a rough, indirect check on their clients' covered work forces in order to guard against what they as a matter of policy would regard as grossly inadequate employer contributions.[3]

Most of the companies interviewed said that they relied on the initiative of their employees and/or the unions, if the employees are organized, to insure the correctness of records. This is a reasonable procedure in the case of contributory pension plans, where accretions are usually reported to employees, or in noncontributory plans of medium- and larger-sized firms which are increasingly following the practice of making annual reports to each employee of his pension accumulation.

In other cases, however, the question arises as to how the employee would know about being either partially or totally overlooked for pension purposes. It apparently does happen in large multiple-company organizations that unintentional gaps sometimes occur in an employee's pension

---

[2] Cf. Chapter VIII.
[3] Cf. Chapter VI.

credit when he is transferred from his company prior to adoption or improvement of the pension plan.

Oversight cases have apparently turned up only very rarely to date. Moreover, they have involved retired employees rather than exited employees with deferred pension rights. There does nevertheless appear to be a "missing link" in the pension administration chain as far as insuring the accuracy of in-firm record keeping is concerned. The problem would appear to extend to all types of pension plans.

Administration of Benefits

The actual granting of pensions to retiring employees would appear to be one of the most permanently held functions in the pension administration field as far as the companies studied were concerned, not only because of the role a company must play in initiating action for retiring employees, but also because of the desire of employers to participate in this function. A few companies were encountered which, apparently because of a felt inability or an indisposition to perform the function, use a pension consultant for this purpose. However, this does not seem to be common, and the other extreme of the company not only awarding the pensions, but also arranging for the first checks to come from the company and/or periodically keeping in touch with the pensioner is much more likely.

The reason for the interest of employers in the pension-award function has nothing to do with any distrust of outside agencies but rather with the favorable image that is thought to be created with continuing employees by this final demonstration of company interest. This is indeed a very favorable omen from the standpoint of pension security. It was stated by a number of employer representatives interviewed that a company which paid out the substantial sums required for pensions and which did not obtain this "personnel mileage" from handing out the pensions itself was utterly foolish. The strength of the feeling is also underscored by the fact that some of the companies interviewed said (rightly or wrongly) they had changed from one funding medium to another among other reasons because they felt that they would appear more important in the granting of pension benefits with their new arrangements.

As has been suggested earlier, it is common practice for the multilocation firm to decentralize to a degree its administration of benefits to the plant level. Usually this means that the retiring employee makes application to the personnel section of his plant (or in some plans to his union also) and is then in an interview told of the recommendation being made for his pension. The point of this is to make the process less impersonal and perfunctory. If there is a union, this is a matter of importance to the union also, which is likely to have had a role or interest in the provision of pension benefits.

Pension Administrators and Boards

One finds either a pension administrator or a board of administration (called also "pension board," "pension committee," etc.) charged with making the ultimate decision on applications for pensions. Boards appear to be more common than single administrators, although it is perhaps significant that two of the companies interviewed said that they had abandoned the board idea in favor of a single administrator on the grounds that this kind of committee did not justify itself. Occasionally a company will have more than one board, usually when there are separate plans for salaried and hourly workers, and often when operations are spread out over several plants.

The typical pension board, when it exists, is likely to include a representative each from the company's financial, personnel, and one of its operating departments, plus two or three representatives from either supervisory or employee ranks (in many negotiated plans the employee representatives are, as might be expected, selected by the union). The practice of including employee representatives receives some advocacy from employers and is not confined to plans negotiated with unions. It is regarded as another means of bringing the company's role in providing pensions home to the employees and therefore desirable, especially when the board's functions are somewhat perfunctory. Also there appears to have been a generally favorable experience with employee representation, including union-selected representatives. In nearly all cases in these single-employer plans, one of the company representatives, very often the financial representative, is chairman and carries out the directives issued by the board.

In most cases the single administrator or the board has as its responsibilities four decision areas—eligibility, relevant service and/or compensation, disability, and post-eligibility violations—these things reflecting the typical structure of contemporary pension plans.[4] In two companies interviewed the boards had authority in investment matters and in the selection of funding agencies, actuary, etc. These responsibilities, however, are to be regarded as exceptional for boards of administration in single-employer plans.

Just how much the boards studied had to say or to add

---

[4] Decisions on posteligibility violations of the conditions of a plan are, as might be expected, less frequent than in the other areas and in no one's recollection involved the invocation of the "moral turpitude" clause in many pension plans. Violations of the prohibition against working for a competitor do come up, however, in such industries as chemicals, electronics, and advertising.

to imposed policy in their areas of responsibility varied greatly. In some cases the boards clearly were expected to make a mechanical interpretation of the pension plan in the areas enumerated and clearly did so. This happened both with negotiated and conventional plans. It seemed true, moreover, that in the case of negotiated plans, including especially those with joint union-management boards of administration, there was more of an attempt by all parties to operate in a mechanical fashion on the theory that the collective bargaining agreement was comprehensive and not to be rewritten by the board. Whether or not the adjective "comprehensive" is a correct one is a question which needs to be considered.

On the other hand, several of the boards which had no union representation quite clearly had been given and were expected to carry out rather important policy-making responsibilities in interpreting eligibility provisions, defining disability, etc. To this end minutes were carefully drawn and filed for reference. While, as with the mechanically operated boards discussed in the preceding paragraph, an annual report on retirements and pensions was prepared for the company board of directors and lines of communication established with company top management and (depending upon the nature of the representation) the union, the difference appeared to be in the frequency with which these lines of communication were exercised. With active boards of administration they were exercised, whereas in the case of mechanically operated boards communications to management were less frequent.[5]

---

[5] Individual board members, whether employer or union (in the case of boards with bipartite representation), of course "wear another hat" and by virtue of this may influence policy through their respective "channels." We are not talking about this here, although this alternative means of action can be an important modifier of board action.

Other boards were uncovered which in the beginning had quite obviously been active but which after the first year of the plan had become essentially perfunctory organs presumably maintained for their employee-relations value rather than for their contribution to administration. Whether this had happened because all problems had been solved or because of a change in the mandate of the group was generally not obvious. There were enough boards in the group encountered to raise the question of whether or not a pattern of early activity and eventual atrophy is the most likely one for boards of administration.

If one were to generalize on the question of the significance of either individual pension administrators or boards of administration in important as opposed to more or less perfunctory decision making, three variables would seem to be crucial. The first of these is the attitude of top management towards delegation of authority. In some of the companies interviewed it was quite obvious that this attitude was the controlling factor, inasmuch as other circumstances (to be discussed directly) were essentially neutral and either centralization or decentralization to the administrator or board was conceivable. Where centralization was the policy, the administrator or board obviously existed for the sake of good employee relations, rather than for decision making.

A second and more important variable is the complexity of the employee and wage classification problems encountered by the company. On the matter first of employee classifications, most pension plans exclude temporary and part-time employees and spell out continuity of service requirements. In some industries characterized by frequent and sometimes extended layoffs of personnel the identification of permanent, full-time employees is not always easy as far as pension administration is concerned. If the mandate of the administra-

tor or board is to be judiciously liberal, as seemed generally
to be the case, quite obviously there are difficult decisions to
be made in these circumstances of irregular employment.[6]

Wage structure complexities become important only
when pension benefit formulae involve the level of compensation. Many plans do incorporate this feature, especially unilateral plans.[7] When this is the case practices of paying
shift differentials, incentive rates, overtime, etc., quite obviously pose special problems from the standpoint of relevant
compensation for pension purposes. If such payments vary
greatly from period to period, and if actuarial assumptions
fail to encompass these variations completely, as is likely to
be the case, important decisions will have to be made by
someone in order to maintain the financial intentions inherent in the pension plan. This sort of question is apparently
given serious consideration by pension boards, especially in
larger companies.

A third variable affecting the activities and general
significance of company pension administrators and boards
is the language of the plan itself. If the plan does not say
how layoffs are to be interpreted, what is the relevant earnings base, how disability is to be evaluated, etc., quite obviously these matters will have to be resolved when and to the
extent that they come up. Many of the plans examined appeared to be brief relative to the companies to which they
pertained. Also it is apparently true, and an explanation of
this brevity, that managements and negotiators, union and
management alike, tend to be more concerned with the level
of theoretical estimates of pension costs than with the as-

---

[6] Internal Revenue regulations are pertinent also, since as a condition of
qualification of pension plans for tax purposes there must be no discrimination
in favor of high-salaried employees of a company.

[7] Cf. Bankers Trust Co., *A Study of Industrial Retirement Plans* (1956
ed.), pp. 17–22.

sumptions and circumstances underlying and affecting these costs, so that questions calling for interpretation and decision should arise, perhaps more frequently than they do in practice.

Significance and Future of Administrative Integration

It seems quite clear that the assumption of pension administration responsibilities by employers, individually and in some cases in conjunction with unions, has its very good features from the standpoint of pension security. However, there are also some areas which quite possibly need reconsideration.

The best feature of the reintegration is the reason for it, namely recognition by employers of the importance in terms of employee relations of being interested in and identified with the granting of pensions to retiring employees. As long as employers feel this way there is strong presumption of the intended security of pension promises and not too much reason to be concerned with the spirit (though not necessarily the substance) of the methods used to implement these promises. This is a point which deserves to be borne in mind, especially in connection with the discussion of financial integration methods in the chapter following.

Among the areas of employer pension administration which show up as needing some reconsideration, the most important is that involving the control of record-keeping procedures which, as has been pointed out, is rather incomplete. This function was apparently rather carefully attended to before the present degree of integration of pension administration into employer personnel work but somehow—perhaps because of progress in record keeping—has dropped out of the picture in most pension situations. It is a function of great import to pension security, especially with developments such as the liberalization of vesting privileges. Whether or not the function is to be exercised by employers or by funding and service agencies, a possibility to be discussed later in this book, it seems quite necessary that employers—and unions, for that matter—recognize the problem.

The importance of these observations on the current situation depends to a very large extent on the continuing activity of employers in the field of pension administration. As was suggested at the outset of this chapter business integration tends not to be constant in its degree over time and is tied up very closely with the assessment by firms of the economics of performing various functions.

One finds it hard to believe that employers will ever want to turn the granting of benefits out of their operations in view of the present and likely importance of good personnel relations. The discovery of the probable value of good personnel relations has been one of the great and difficult achievements of modern business administration.

Similarly one doubts that any well-run firm would let policy making in pension administration matters lapse. Although there is evidence suggested by the atrophying of some pension boards that this has happened in some cases, the spread of knowledge on the role of well-timed policy making in good management is likely to be a determining factor in counteracting this development.

By the same token one might expect some of the operations in pension administration currently carried on by employers to be contracted out to service agencies in the future for economic reasons. Record keeping and processing for pension purposes is probably a good example. In the case of all but very large employers these operations will probably be found to be economically done in a highly mechanized fashion which is possible only in large volume cases. The impact from the standpoint of pension security should be expected to be good, given the difficulties which employers seem to have had with this operation doing it themselves. However, the outcome will also be influenced by the effect of contracting out the operation on the employer's ability to use and interpret the data returned to him for intelligent administration. This is the usual problem connected with specialized information development for management decision making.

Chapter IV

OPERATION OF SINGLE-EMPLOYER PLANS: FINANCIAL MANAGEMENT BY EMPLOYERS

Extent and Organization of Financial Integration

In financial matters it was found that most large-, medium- and small-sized employers have in various ways come to consider the financial aspects of their pension plans in conjunction with their broader enterprise financial planning. This attitude and the practices which accompany it we refer to as "financial integration." In general, firms with newer initial pension plans do less of this than firms which have had pension plans operating for longer periods of time. Beyond this, however, it is difficult to generalize about which firms integrate the most. The technical form of administration is not reflective of integration policies, i.e., a plan which does not use corporate trustees or an insurance company is not necessarily one whose financial management is most closely integrated into the affairs of the sponsoring firm. In one important case of this sort, for example, most matters relating directly and indirectly to money appeared to be kept strictly separate from the normal financial activities of the firm. This was not the case in a number of plans studied which were insured or technically bank trusteed.

Also it is to be stressed that there are many areas of

possible action by employers besides the much discussed management of investment portfolios.[1] Some of the more important of these areas of action are (1) the choice of a funding agency, (2) the amount of the annual contribution to a bank or insurance company, and (3) revision of actuarial and accounting procedures used in valuations. Internal Revenue regulations for qualification of pension plans have certain restrictions, notably in the matter of overfunding.[2] They do, however, leave substantial room for financial maneuver by employers.

The person or persons who would normally be expected to play a leading role in a company's pension affairs, given the assertions made above, would be the company treasurer or chief financial officer and his assistants. This turned out to be almost uniformly true with the companies interviewed, where the company was big enough to have an active management level below the president. There were a few exceptional instances, one where pension functions had been pulled out of other departments and put under a man whose background nevertheless was in his company's treasury department, two others where personnel executives had attained organizational status superior to that of their financial colleagues in pension matters, and one other, a large company with a committee management tradition, where the financial and personnel people were of equal status.

By and large, however, the chief financial executive and his assistants turned out to be senior to other functional and operating executives in the day-to-day work of management. The implication of this fact for the significance of employer

---

[1] See, for example, State of New York, Insurance Department, *Private Employee Benefit Plans—A Public Trust*, submitted by Martin S. House, Special Counsel (1956).

[2] Cf. Edwin W. Patterson, *Legal Protection of Private Pension Expectations* (Homewood, Ill.: Richard D. Irwin, Inc., 1960), chap. iii.

financial management in private pension plans is underscored by the additional fact that in a healthy minority of the cases studied the information was volunteered that recent reorganizations had put the management of pensions exclusively or substantially more within the purview of the company's financial officers.

Funding Agencies and Methods

The funding agencies which might be used for pension plans for various reasons lend themselves in differential fashion to a policy of integrating the financial aspects of a pension plan with a company's total financial picture. Hence, one naturally wants to know whether or not this fact has figured in the choice of funding agencies by employers in any significant way. There was little indication in the information supplied by the companies interviewed that this was the case, although we are somewhat handicapped here from not having asked the question directly.[3]

In most of the interviews information was volunteered that the funding arrangement had been chosen for other reasons. Opinions as to the differential rates of investment accretion of funds under different funding media were offered most frequently. Also there was some evaluation of security that was thought to characterize the different funding media. Finally a few firms had obviously been thinking in terms of both of these frames of reference and wanted arrangements which they thought would satisfy both in some optimal way.

It would appear that the kind of financial flexibility— particularly as regards the amount of the employer's annual contribution—which is possible using some funding media under the terms offered by some funding agencies has not

---

[3] See Appendix—"Client Company Questionnaire."

been a primary consideration typically thus far in the initial choice of a funding agency. To some extent one could of course draw a different conclusion from reading the promotional literature put out by some of the funding agencies and seeing what might be called the "concessions" offered in the matter of funding. However, the writer considers it significant that the agencies which he has in mind are not the "big operators" among the funding institutions.

As will be implicit in the following discussion, any flexibility which happens to characterize the arrangements with the funding agency chosen will be used by a company which for one reason or another develops a cash problem. However, this is quite a different thing from deliberately choosing a particular agency for this potentiality.

Contribution Rates and Consequences

As was pointed out in the preceding section of this report the board of directors typically makes the initial decisions concerning the structure of a company's pension plan and oversees changes, including changes in funding arrangements. One additional operating area always handled by the board is the company's annual contribution to the pension fund. This could be a perfunctory decision and by some standards of actuarial soundness certainly should be, except for small adjustments due to mortality experience, turnover where it is pertinent, and possibly interest earnings, once a pension plan with a funding program has been drawn up.[4]

The indications are, however, that the decision on size of contribution is not a perfunctory one and may be regarded typically as a true variable in the operation of pension plans.

---

[4] See, for example, the excellent review of the subject in Dorrance C. Bronson, *Concepts of Actuarial Soundness in Pension Plans* (Homewood, Ill.: Richard D. Irwin, Inc., 1957), chap. x.

While no "hard" data were obtained and analyzed here, it was made quite clear in a number of instances that the amount of the annual contribution had been varied in accordance with the total financial picture and needs of the respective companies.

In some instances, where contributions were reduced because of cash shortage or cash needs, the action is direct and stated as a deviation from original funding plans. In other instances the reduction in contribution is asserted to be the result of favorable experience, usually in the area of earnings on investment, and is taken in conjunction with either a prior change in investment portfolio or else a change in accounting and/or actuarial valuation procedures.

Such indirection certainly does not constitute dissimulation or an illicit act, as long as dissimulation is not intended and as long as the procedures used are consistent with originally conservative funding plans and with each other in time. Indeed much can be said from a security as well as management standpoint for keeping outlays in operating areas of a business in line with the fortunes of a business and for keeping these outlays co-ordinated with the capital needs of the business over time. Both of these areas are often not well attended to and as a result the long-term position of the firm is impeded. This usually means that jobs and pensions are put in jeopardy.

Investment Management by Employers

The extent to which employers attempt to participate in the investment decisions made imperative by their pension contributions turns out to be one of the most difficult things to estimate in the whole financial management area. It seems quite clear that if our sampling of practice is at all representative previous inquiries into this subject underestimate the extent of the participation. Perhaps this is because these previous inquiries have been based primarily upon the language of bank indenture agreements. It seems quite clear also that incidents of self-dealing investment demands by employers and other shady practices are not important as a practical matter and probably not possible in most pension situations.[5]

Beyond these broad generalizations, however, precisely what goes on in the way of investment management and influence by employers cannot be described in any summary fashion. Some of the firms interviewed quite frankly and, in the case of large firms, publicly, have pension funds which may or may not have a corporate trustee and which are administered by the firms themselves. In the case of the large firms such management is delegated to a treasurer or assistant treasurer with a staff, and these people handle the investment portfolio within the policy framework laid down for them by top management, of which the treasurer is often an important member.

When smaller firms do their own management the manager seems often to be the president or some board member with a penchant for investment management. Some of the banks claim that the latter sort of arrangement tends to be a temporary one: the employer executive eventually finds that he is unable, either because of a lack of time or else because of lack of training, to do a good job.

At the other end of the spectrum the writer was told with apparent candor in some of his interviews that investment matters were considered to be out of the province of company management and were to be left completely to the funding agency. Employers who seemed to mean what they said here, e.g., through the accounts they gave of the nature

---

[5] Cf. Chapter VI.

and frequency of their contacts with their bank trustees, were relatively few in the group of companies interviewed for this study. In general they seemed also to be smaller companies with relatively new pension plans.

In between these two extremes of complete employer investment management and complete abnegation of the responsibility for investment was, in the present investigation, the majority. Of this group all indicated that they had worked out a broad portfolio policy for and with the bank trustee when the bank was used as the funding agency. The nature of the policies developed varied with the financial attitudes of the companies and their banks, the payout expectations of the plan, the funding rate, and the existence or nonexistence of a split-funding arrangement which may provide a dual source of payout funds.

As is well known, it is quite common for a sponsoring employer to take a position in regard to purchases by a trusteed fund of the employer's securities. Such provisions were characteristic of most of the plans studied, although there were a number of instances of advocacy rather than prohibition of purchase. Some of the larger firms studied apparently have also deemed it necessary to insert prohibitions against the purchase of competitors' common stock and against excessive purchases of any company's securities in order to stay at peace with the Antitrust Division of the U.S. Department of Justice.

A basically more potent, though on the surface rather passive, instrument of influence on the investment activities of funding agencies is the review, usually, in the case of bank-trusteed plans, a quarterly review, of the performance of the fund. (In the case of insured plans, particular attention is paid also to "better" treatment in experience ratings.) Whether because of the encouragement seemingly offered by most banks to such reviews or more probably because of the interest in financial integration which has been discussed above, this review by employer boards of directors and their operating financial management seldom seemed to be perfunctory.

In most of the instances where the writer was told that the funding agencies were left to their own devices once the initial arrangements were made, he was also told of the existence of this review process. When the report from a bank trustee is being considered the practice is for the board to raise questions, not only about general performance and policy, but also about particular investments. Obviously the perceptive trustee will take note of these questions and the investment preferences which seem to underlie them. Whether or not he will adjust to these preferences is a matter which will be discussed in Chapter VI.

Occasionally this questioning will also lead to action by the employer board. In one instance the writer was told of an enraged board which issued a prohibition against the purchase of stock of a competitor who was thought by the board to be inferior. In another instance the trustee was asked to substitute a dividend-paying stock for a very highly regarded growth stock.

Instances of cashiering a particular bank trustee or insurance company (whose representative presumably will take note of the attitude towards the dividend rate) for performance reasons are apparently rare.[6] However, with the growth of split funding it is indicated both by the companies using this arrangement and by the banks and insurance companies participating as funding agencies that the weapon of chang-

---

[6] In the case of the review process applied to insured plans, the effect of questioning apparently has been most directly felt recently in the demand from the group departments of many insurance companies for a change in the method of allocating investment income, as will be discussed later in Chapter VI.

ing the relative shares of the funding participants has been used and will be used increasingly in the future.

A final and much more ephemeral form of informal pressure from the sponsoring employer on the investment policies of the funding agency seems likely to arise from the day-to-day conversations between the funding agency representative and the liaison man in the sponsoring firm. This is easiest to discuss and probably much more relevant in the case of bank-trusteed plans, both because of the nature of the arrangement and also because the banks have apparently encouraged this kind of contact.

What is said to happen in these conversations, whether or not required under the terms of the trust agreement, is that the bank trustee informs the liaison man, usually a financial officer of the company, of the current investment operations of the trust fund. The liaison man is likely to have a reaction and will be listened to, if only because of his potential influence on the client's attitude towards its funding agency. It is very difficult to follow through with the analysis from here. However, in some cases it was quite clear that the liaison man was effectively "calling the shots."

An example of the difficulties inherent in estimating employer influence processes of the type discussed is suggested by the following comparison encountered in the investigation. On the one hand, we have the relevant passage from the trust instrument between an employer sponsoring a plan and the bank trustee:

The Trustee shall invest and reinvest the principal and income of the Fund and keep the same invested without distinction between principal and income in any kind of property, real or personal, including common and preferred stocks and units or shares of any Diversified or Common Trust Fund managed or operated by the Trustee and without at any time being limited to such classes of investments as may from time to time be designated as legal investments for fiduciaries in [this state] or elsewhere: provided, however, that the Trustee shall submit to the Company for approval its recommendations concerning *general policy* for making and altering investments in advance of the inauguration or change of any such policy and upon certification of such approval the Trustee shall be fully protected in any action which is taken within the scope of the policy so approved and which is taken with the same prudence which it would ordinarily exercise in the investment of its own funds.[7]

In the interview it was learned that the bank trustee checks out every purchase or sale of a security in the company's fund with an employer executive acting as liaison man. This practice suggests a somewhat more detailed association between the employer and the trustee than is called for in the trust agreement. The company in question happens to have an investment counselor advising on its pension fund investments, in addition to the bank. In this instance there is a rule to the effect that the company requires the bank and the investment counselor to agree, as well as to get its approval, on all portfolio changes.

While the extent of employer participation in the investment management activities of the funding agencies is suggested by the preceding discussion, the motives are less clear except in two or three rather overt acts which were reported. It is probably safe to presume that in the case of initial policies affecting portfolios and rates of accretion in principal, as well as in periodic directives concerning these things, the object is to integrate the behavior of the pension fund with the general needs anticipated in the pension plan and with the financial condition of the sponsoring company.

The day-to-day contacts are harder to explain, except insofar as they are a means used by the funding agencies to

---

[7] The name of the state has been deleted for reasons of confidence. Emphasis has been added by the writer.

maintain their position with their clients.[8] Certainly these contacts promote understanding, which can be very important in getting appropriate investment arrangements, and also probably provide information to the funding agencies.

On the other hand, one wonders if this degree of contact is actually necessary from the standpoint of effective integration, except in those apparently few instances where employer contributions are made monthly. It would seem as if the policy and review procedures discussed above would suffice. Also, observing the variation in knowledge of investments among employers and the consternation caused among the funding agencies by some requests made for them, one wonders if both the employers and the funding agencies are in some degree asking for trouble by encouraging a very detailed working relationship between persons who are not always professional equals. The preceding statement of course is not meant to apply to cases where the employer or his representative happen to be experienced and successful in this field of investment management or where, as in the case example given, the employer has seen fit to bring in additional competent counsel.

Actuarial and Accounting Revisions

While the preceding discussion of investment management activities of employers has been detailed and long because of its complexity, there is yet another area in which employers have apparently become increasingly interested and active as part of their financial overseeing of pension activities. This area encompasses the actuarial and accounting assumptions made in connection with the valuation of pension fund assets and liabilities. The action involves the

---

[8] See Chapter VI.

co-ordination of practice with the financial position of the firm.

In the matter of liabilities, it is being recognized that under the law these can (and should) be revalued in accordance with changes in work force composition, turnover (unless there is immediate and complete vesting), mortality experience, wage progression experience, and the rate of interest and capital accretion of the pension fund. In addition, such matters as the rate of funding of past service liability and the procedure for funding future service liability are widely argued to be very much within the realm of financial judgment and therefore are, within the limits of Internal Revenue regulation, a responsibility of management to manage. As was pointed out to the writer, pension outlays made without consideration of anything but some arbitrarily chosen funding plan are likely to be excessive in terms of true cost because of a failure to relate them to the varying financial position of the firm; that is to say, they can be cheap or dear depending on how much money the firm has to spend at the time of the outlay and upon its other financial requirements.

With respect to valuation of assets in the financial audit of a pension plan, it is well known that accountants prefer to use the same basis for valuation over time in order to provide such comparability of their data as is considered essential for comprehension. On the other hand, it has also been pointed out very frequently that accounting procedures serving one purpose, such as financial reporting on a comparable basis, may not serve other purposes, notably those involving effective resource allocation by the firm.[9] In the field of pension accounting in particular valuation of fund

---

[9] Cf. B. Goetz, *Management Planning and Control* (New York: McGraw-Hill Book Co., Inc., 1949).

assets at cost in a rising market understates the current market valuation of these assets, unless or until there is a compensating decline in market values. The required contribution by a company in any one year is thus overstated. This fact has also been noted by employers.

The foregoing observations on actuarial and accounting valuation procedures have evidently led increasingly to a demand by many employers for periodic revisions of their pension fund assets and liabilities. Most of the demands seem to be correlated with the broad indices of business conditions. However, it has happened, presumably in view of recent federal monetary management aimed at inflation, that companies also ask for such revisions in order to release cash for expansion in prosperous times.

These rather sophisticated manifestations of the trend towards weaving pension affairs into the total financial strategy of the firm sponsoring the pension plan are closely related to the actions discussed earlier, of many employers in varying the amount of the annual contribution in light of the current financial picture for the firm. There is, however, the important difference here that the concepts of asset and liability as they apply to pension plans to some extent are being made functions of the venture position of the sponsoring firm.

This is a somewhat different approach than has been customary. Whether a conflict of interest arises as between management for stockholders and management for pension plan members is not at once clear. If pensioners had to forego or wait for their pensions as the result of revaluations for purposes of financial strategy, there indeed would be the strong presumption of a conflict of interest. There was, however, no evidence that this has happened in the case of companies insisting on revaluations. Hence, the matter of conflict of interest is not clear since revaluation practices can be interpreted as a contributory factor to pension adequacy and security in circumstances where the pensioners must rely ultimately on the well-being of an employer.

Summary and Evaluation

Aside from certain specific points, notably the day-to-day contacts among employers and their funding agencies, the whole set of financial management activities of employers bearing on pensions which has been discussed in this section can be viewed with alarm or favorably, depending upon one's general attitude towards the mechanisms which we have been discussing in this chapter. If one believes in and trusts the official role of the private enterprise firm as the allocator of resources in an economy such as we have, then, except for specific instances of wrongdoing or incompetence, he can only look with approval on the resourcefulness of business enterprises managing their pension affairs along the lines which have been outlined. If, on the other hand, one associates security in private pensions with a particular form of financial behavior by employers, then he will be deeply disturbed by the opportunities for and practices of financial maneuver for the sake of weaving pension costs into the financial needs and plans of the firm whose managers are of course subject to other influences besides those of their employees.

As far as recent and current experience is concerned, there seems to have been rather a sparsity of great pension disasters connected with the various practices being pursued by employers in the financing of their pension programs. This could be because of the "youth" of many private pension plans characterized by such practices and the conditions of high level business activity which have generally prevailed in the United States since World War II, or because of the presence of other institutional forces (beside the Internal Revenue Service) which have restrained gross mismanagement and malpractice by employers. On the other hand, it seems clear that we have here in the subject of financial management, an area for further questioning. There seems a need for the development of criteria to provide guidance on the question of how much freedom and restriction in financial management is desirable from the standpoint of meeting various social objectives including especially pension security.

However, before we attempt to draw any conclusions of this sort it seems appropriate that we give some attention to the funding and service agencies in the pension field to see what standards pertinent to the subject of pension security these agencies have been able to develop and enforce. Such investigations have constituted an important part of the present study and will be reported on presently after a consideration of multiple-employer plans in the next chapter.

Chapter V

MULTIPLE-EMPLOYER PLANS

Comparison with Single-Employer Plans

Pension plans which are financed by a number of employers as part of a collective bargaining contract with a union and under the provisions of the Taft-Hartley Act[1] require the performance of all of the functions implicit in single-employer plans. Initially a multiple-employer plan has to be structured with respect to such basic characteristics as coverage, benefit formula, contribution system, vesting provisions, if any, etc. Funding arrangements have to be made, contributions forwarded, records of service and earnings, when these are pertinent to benefits, kept, funds managed, and benefits granted and paid. In terms of the general nature of the tasks involved there are no differences between multiple- and single-employer plans, although, as will be suggested, some of these tasks are harder to perform in the typical multiple-employer plan situation.

There are, however, great differences between the two types of pension plans as far as authority relationships are concerned and in the matter of who performs the functions

---

[1] The occasional union pension fund, not financed directly by employer contributions and therefore not under the jurisdiction of the Taft-Hartley Act is excluded from the discussion of this section. We also exclude unilateral multiple-employer plans from the discussion. Many of the plans which we do include, as is well known, actually predate the Taft-Hartley Act by many years.

necessary to provide pensions. The foundation stone as well as the image of these differences is the board of trustees set up to run the plan in collective bargaining between the union and the several employers involved. These boards, which contain equal employer and union representation as well as a provision for an impartial arbitrator, are authoritative as far as the handling of pension affairs is concerned after contribution rates to the plan have been agreed upon.[2] They must perform or have agents (who may not receive compensation if they are employees of one of the employers or officials of the union) carry out all of the functions enumerated above as essential to the provision of pensions. They may at their discretion change the terms of the pension plan. This discretion does not extend to the amount of employer contributions, which is determined through collective bargaining, but does include benefit levels, service requirements, priorities at termination, etc.

Generally speaking the authority to change the terms of the plan is not exercised frequently. All parties appear to have taken the position that board policies should be consistent with the collective bargaining agreements and negotiations which have resulted in the pension plan. It happens, however, that terms are changed in multiple-employer plans when the major employers involved execute new bargaining agreements with the union. When this happens some multi-operation employers, who are engaged primarily in other activities or locations and with other unions, are effectively in the position of having plan terms changed without their prior certification in collective bargaining. For such employers this can indeed be a problem, as one might gather from the material presented in Chapter II.

It is clear from the preceding discussion that multiple-
_____
[2] Cf. Sec. 302 of the Taft-Hartley Act (Public Law 101—80th Congress).

employer plans also differ in their approach to pension planning. The rate of employer contribution is the main subject of initial planning and also of later revisions. This point was noted by employer representatives who were interviewed and has a number of implications which will be discussed presently. For the moment the point of interest is that in the case of multiple-employer plans, given the emphasis on pension contributions and costs, promised benefit levels may be more in the realm of hope than of commitment (which of course is not to say that the hopes may not be fulfilled). The employer's technical responsibility very definitely ends with his living up to his contribution promises, and many employers participating in multiple-employer plans evidently look at it this way. Given the problems connected with making actuarial estimates, and given this sort of commitment (albeit often a weak one) on benefits, a downgrading of the status of pension promises made in multiple-employer plans seems not beyond the realm of possibility.[3]

The implications for pension security of this state of affairs are obviously modified somewhat by the existence of an important third party, i.e., the union, which will presumably attempt to attend to any financial problems of meeting pension obligations in collective bargaining negotiations. This point is also relevant to the impact of the practices discussed in Chapter III, in the case of negotiated single-employer plans. Since the militancy of a union with respect to pension matters is said to vary with such things as the age distribution of the union membership, these third party effects may be variable too, however.

---

[3] It has been suggested that because of the haggling in collective bargaining over cents per hour to be contributed by employers many pension plans of the multiple-employer variety tend to operate on a "pay-as-you-go" basis. Cf. State of New York, Insurance Department, *Private Employee Benefit Plans— A Public Trust*, submitted by Martin S. House, Special Counsel (1956), p. 88.

Another rather unclassifiable but probably compensating difference from the standpoint of the pension security question is underscored by the reaction of a multiple-employer plan administrator to what he regarded as the brevity of the writer's two-hour interview. The administrator said that he had gotten accustomed to inspections lasting two or three weeks during which time every aspect of the operation of the plan was investigated exhaustively. As has been suggested in Chapter II, there is no such counterpart in the case of the single-employer plan.

Activities of Multiple-Employer Plan Trustees

At the outset of a multiple-employer plan and apparently for about the first year of its existence, the trustees are very busy. A plan for the disposition of contributions in excess of payouts has to be worked out. This typically involves a substantial number of interviews with and perusal of brochures offered by interested funding groups.[4] Also an actuary must be hired, and the administration of records and benefits must be provided for in terms both of personnel and procedure. Finally, as the first pension cases come through policy decisions have to be made on matters not provided for specifically in the collective bargaining agreement. From other experience the writer would venture the guess that the list of problems not covered by the typical agreement would be rather lengthy. This notion, however, was not agreed to generally by the people interviewed.

After the first year of the existence of the plan the pace of activity for the board of trustees apparently slackens considerably, so that some boards meet as infrequently as once every six months. Some meet a good deal more often, especially when the board elects to play a rather active part

---

[4] It apparently is not uncommon to ask for bids from funding agencies.

in the management of investments. When this is not the case there seems often to be the feeling, as with the administrative boards of some single-employer plans, that operations can be routinized and delegated to an administrative agent. One of the most interesting things to the writer was the indication received from both union and employer sources that disagreements among the two groups represented on boards of multiple-employer plans are relatively infrequent.

Participation by Employer and Union Representatives

It has been reported that the employer representatives on some Taft-Hartley trustee boards are relatively inactive in the affairs of these boards and allow the union representatives to manage things. Actually this situation seems to be relatively uncommon, especially when the industry or area covered by the plan includes firms of medium and large size. Such firms are likely to have professionally oriented management. These firms usually get themselves elected to the trustee board, or else, if they happen not to be a major factor in the industry or area encompassed by the plan, support the firms which happen to be major factors. Having done so they are not disposed to be and are not, in fact, inactive.

This is not to say that a large number of employers will be active in the management of pension affairs in industries and areas having multiple-employer plans. There seems to be this problem in the multiple-employer type of pension arrangement: many employers who are not also employer representatives on the board of trustees do not identify themselves with pension affairs beyond making the contributions required of them. Feeling this way they are not likely to be concerned with questions of administration and financial management which may have important bearing on the future fulfillment of pension promises.

It does appear to be true that once an employer has become active, presumably through election to the board of trustees, he is likely to continue his interest. Thus greater rotation of trusteeships may be the means for stimulating employer interest. A case in point may be the resistance by active employers which the writer understands is taking place in regard to the efforts of some national unions to amalgamate the several multiple-employer funds in which they participate. These employers feel that they will lose the active role which they would like to have, by virtue of the greater exclusiveness of a "superboard" of trustees.

Even when both employer and management representatives on the board of trustees of a multiple-employer plan are active in the deliberations of the board there tend nevertheless to be areas of special competence for each group. These special talents seem generally to be accepted and used by the whole board, unless the board happens to be one which relies very heavily on a third party. A frequent example is said to arise when the employer representatives are knowledgeable in the field of investments. Here, when investment activity is being carried on by a board of trustees, the employer representatives have great influence in these matters. Similarly the union representatives, often the business agents for the locals participating in the plan, are likely to have considerable knowledge of and contact with employees and employers participating in the plan and in the best of circumstances make an important contribution to problems involving this sort of information.

One very important such instance arises in the matter of preventing default in contributions by employers. A failure by some employers to contribute or to keep up with contributions affects the solvency of the pension fund. Also such a failure is likely to dilute the effectiveness of contributions by employers in good standing. The dilution will be caused by the fact that pensions are to be paid on the basis of years spent in service with participating employers who presumably will contribute in proportion to service done with them. If contributions are not made by some employers, the pension will come from the contributions of other employer participants who in addition to covering service in their own firms will be covering service done for defaulting employers.

In this sort of situation the union trustees are of key importance. While in some cases the task of uncovering defaults is delegated to an independent administrator the union representatives on the board are relied upon to arrange for the manpower and also the strategy for bringing delinquent employers up to date on their contributions.

The Role of Outside Agencies

Outside agencies are perhaps more important to the functioning of multiple-employer pension plans than they are in the case of single-employer plans. For one thing it is obviously neither possible nor desirable to integrate the several administrative and financial functions which must be performed into the affairs of individual employers. Another factor is that the pool of skills necessary for running a pension plan is not likely to be fully and readily available to the board of trustees of a multiple-employer plan. There are some exceptional cases of course, as in the garment trades, where the union is both equipped and disposed to provide many of the services needed and considers the work of the pension plan as its own.

It seems to be the typical situation that a particular third party—an actuary, a consultant, or possibly an attorney—will "father" the pension plan and board in the early stages of their operation. This person or firm will provide advice on a variety of important subjects, including funding alternatives, administrative procedures, relationships with the funding and service agencies chosen by the board. He may in addition take over some of the administrative and financial activities required for the operation of the plan. If he does not do this, he will find persons to do this work in the employ of the board and supervise them in their tasks.

Once operations have been set up the third party often recedes somewhat into the background as far as decisions by the board of trustees are concerned. This recession, however, is likely to be less than with single-employer plans, where, it was suggested earlier, the initial superior role of an outside consultant who helps the company board of directors structure the pension plan tends to be taken over by operating management within the company. In addition, there appear to be a number of cases in the multiple-employer field where the third party continues either through his own inclinations and salesmanship or by the wishes of the trustee board to be the dominant actor in the operation of the plan.

In instances where such continued activity by the third party occurs, it might be surmised that financial problems, engendered either by the contemplated investment activities of the board of trustees, or else by financial difficulties encountered by firms participating in the plan and affecting their contributions, are of great importance. And so it happens that not uncommonly consultants and actuaries to multiple-employer plans, while nominally advising on actuarial and purely administrative matters, play an advisory role also in matters related to the investment activities of the plan. In one case known to the writer the consultant has been very active in a number of ways in cutting the costs of investment management of plans where a bank trustee is used. In some other cases consultants have or are planning to combine with investment advisory and funding firms, presumably to provide this kind of service in one package along with actuarial and administrative services. Developments of this sort will be discussed in Chapter VII.

The activities of the consultant in circumstances of employer stress also appear to encompass the consideration of measures designed to "bail out" the employer and thereby to maintain his existence. While this work could be very far-reaching, generally speaking financial advice is the consultant's main stock in trade in the employer in difficulty. Attempting to arrange for loans from fund assets to distressed employers in the plan is apparently not beyond the scope of activities of some consultants who, presumably for reasons of loyalty to the idea of pension plans in multiple-employer circumstances or business or both, will leave no stone unturned in the matter of preserving the plan. How frequently loans from the fund are made was not ascertained, and, because of the questions the practice raises, would be worthy of further study.

Beyond these reasons for the relative maintenance of third-party activity in multiple-employer plans after the plans are in operation, such factors, noted above, as the impossibility of integrating multiple-employer plans into the affairs of member firms and lack of necessary skills directly available are likely to be continuing problems for the multiple-employer plan. The farthest most boards of trustees go in providing for their own staff seems to be in the field of record keeping which is the primary and in one sense sole function of the hired administrator.[5] Other services, if they

---

[5] In some cases which were encountered by the writer, however, the paid administrator was quite clearly in the process of expanding his role at the expense of the primary outside consultant. The latter were usually aware of this and were resisting, which may be a significant commentary on the importance of the several reasons cited here for the maintenance of third-party activity.

cannot be borrowed, as sometimes happens in the case of legal advice gotten from union counsel or from employer members with legal training, must be provided by third parties—the funding agencies or the service groups. Quite naturally these third parties will continue to be something of an active force in the operation of multiple-employer plans.

Educational Activities by Third Parties

In this context it is of some interest that funding and service agencies working with multiple-employer plans apparently undertake to provide much more of what might be described as "education" to their trustee clients. By its nature and organization the multiple-employer board provides a ready and, to a certain extent, desirous sort of "open forum" for such activities. The boards of trustees are, after all, quasi-public bodies. Also, while many of the individual trustees may not have had prior training in the decision areas encompassed by the board, these trustees nevertheless are supposed to participate in their board's decisions and presumably be able to give an explanation of why they voted as they did to their sponsoring unions and employers and quite possibly to public bodies.

Probably for these reasons many of the consultants operating in the multiple-employer field appear to have developed much more in the way of educational information on pension planning and operation than those consultants servicing single-employer clients. Presumably the informational materials put out are for the edification of all interested parties.

The funding agencies also seem to take much greater pains in the education of their multiple-employer clients through active attendance at trustee board meetings. It is of course true that representatives of funding agencies would probably not be admitted to the deliberations of the governing agencies in single-employer plans except occasionally and through very special invitation. Some of the funding people talked to tended to be a little cynical about the activities of competitors in the case of multiple-employer plans. However, the actuality of these measures is not to be overlooked, since they can be helpful from the standpoint of pension security as well as misleading, which is the charge of the critics.

Evaluation

If one were to consider the strengths and weaknesses of the multiple-employer type of pension plan from the standpoint of pension security there would be items in each category. On the side of strengths first is the diversity of viewpoint which is allowed and required to operate on the affairs of a multiple-employer plan if it is of the Taft-Hartley variety, and most of them are. As will become clear in succeeding chapters, single-employer plans are in reality not as divorced from the influence of outside agencies as their mode of operation suggests at first sight. Also some multiple-employer plans are to a considerable extent tied in with the operations of the sponsoring union. Nevertheless a degree of protection against subordination of the affairs of the plan to any one viewpoint is built into the multiple-employer plan.

This may conceivably be an illusory advantage when we recall that many trustee boards tend to become relatively inactive after the first year or so of operation of their plan and also when we recall the continued dominance of outside agencies in the affairs of some boards. Also the fact that trustee boards have apparently tended to work harmoniously to date does not prove that they can work in circumstances of substantial internal conflict if this happens in the future. Nonetheless there is technically a law against monopoly in the operation of multiple-employer plans.

Another advantage of the multiple-employer type of plan is likely to be its scale of operations. In all probability, this scale brings lower administrative costs exclusive of record keeping (which would be duplicated) than would be possible for many participating firms operating single-employer plans, especially if the participating firms were relatively small. Specialization and increased bargaining power with service agencies are likely to be the causes.

Finally, various pension reciprocity arrangements which appear to be developing among multiple-employer plans have favorable connotations from the standpoint of pension security. The effect of such reciprocity is to provide to a degree the advantages of vested pensions, although, of course, the covered number must stay within the reciprocity area.

On the other hand, there are some bothersome features about the multiple-employer type of pension plan. In the opinion of the writer the most important of these is the divorcement in most respects of pension affairs from management activities of many employers who after haggling over the amount of the contribution in collective bargaining negotiations recede from or, by virtue of the representation system, are prevented from remaining in the pension picture. There is little incentive in such an arrangement to feel responsible morally for employee pensions, and many employers in multiple-employer plans evidently do not. The union with whom the plan was developed is of course a potential source of ultimate protection to employee participants and pensioners. However, the "cents per hour" approach to the bargaining of pensions which has been discussed raises the question of the amount of protection which in reality obtains.

One might also raise a question about the influence wielded on multiple-employer plans by outside advisory agencies. These agencies were seen to be virtually required adjuncts of the multiple-employer plan in such fields as record keeping and administration. And they have been clearly catalytic influences in the effectuation of multiple-employer pension plans of the Taft-Hartley variety. On the other hand, they appear often to be dominant in the operation of plans and as such make themselves vulnerable from a conflict of interest standpoint.

The solution to the first problem which involves individual employer interest in the pension plan may well be found in employer representation systems which emphasize rotation in participation on the trustee board. However, this must not lead to a weakening of employer influence. As far as the second problem is concerned, a proper balance of influence, as between the trustees of a multiple-employer plan and outside advisory agencies, seems best a function of time and self-education rather than rules and regulations.

Chapter VI

FUNDING AGENCIES AND FINANCIAL ADVISORS

Historical Note: Organization of Section

Having traced the operations and policies of the sponsors of private pension plans, we now turn to a consideration of what has been referred to at the outset of this report as the "pension industry"—in this chapter the funding agencies and financial advisors, and in subsequent chapters service and consulting agencies. As has been suggested, this transfer of attention is not only desirable from the standpoint of getting a full knowledge of the alternatives available for the implementation of pension ideas but also of the context in which pension activities highly integrated into the affairs of their sponsors operate. With regard to the matter of context, the important question is the degrees to which the several types of pension funding and service agencies have influenced and been influenced by employers and unions sponsoring pension plans.

As is well known the insurance companies, or at least some of them, have been for a long time a significant factor in the funding branch (as well as in other branches) of the private pension industry. Banks functioning as corporate trustees have come into a position of perhaps greater importance currently. Investment counselors, while still rela-

64

tively unimportant in the pension field numerically, have apparently gained a share of the investment management business of the banks, and almost concurrently it would seem the mutual funds have become a visible factor in the funding picture as a funding vehicle for private pensions.

It is perhaps a bit unorthodox to consider the agencies just enumerated in one breath, as it were, if only because they are so diverse in their origins and current functions. On the other hand, they are the major participants in what is probably the most important area of competition in the pension field today. Also, as will be suggested below, they appear to be becoming more rather than less competitive with each other. An exception seems to arise in certain areas, where seemingly, through the influence of the preferences of pension clients, some sort of *modus vivendi* has been achieved.

In the sections which follow we shall first review pertinent data concerning the operations of insurance companies, banks, investment counselors, and mutual funds in the pension field. Then an attempt will be made to characterize the competition among them and, following this, to assess the relationship between operations and competition. All of this will be with the final object in mind of saying something about the impact of the funding agencies and financial advisors in their present states on the security of private pensions.

Insurance Company Operations

At the present time insurance companies operating in the private pension field engage themselves to various degrees in six main functions relating to their pension clients—sales, record keeping, actuarial work, investment, special service (employee communications work in particular), and legal forms. Most sales of pension plans are achieved through agents and brokers rather than directly, so that the function handled by the insurance company itself is a management one, by and large, except, of course, for pension plan design service done by the insurance company. The legal service function as far as the client is concerned is apparently also limited, in this case to the design of plans and contracts. When the client already has a pension plan, the activity of designing the plan document is increasingly restricted and turned over to the client's attorneys.

The functions of record keeping, in the matter of active lives and also in the matter of keeping up with deferred and actual annuitants, actuarial service, and investment are probably to be regarded as the key functional areas of insurance company operation in the pension field. The employee communication and education function is seemingly carried on by insurance companies because of a service requirement of this sort from some employers. Except for supervision of what these communications have to say about the responsibility of the insurance company, the latter does not consider this function as a primary one.

Despite the traditional importance of record keeping and actuarial work in pension operations of insurance companies, it does appear that these two functions are dropping somewhat in the frequency of their association with insurance company operations in the pension field. A case in point is, of course, the deposit administration type of group annuity contract where, somewhat to the chagrin of the insurance companies, the recording of active lives for whom the employer contribution is made and the actuarial work involved in setting up the accompanying pension plan may at the option of the sponsoring employer be carried on by parties foreign to the insurance company. This option is apparently taken up in a good number of cases.

In conventional group annuity contracts, too, as was noted in Chapter III, the insurance companies have for some time in many cases apparently not exercised their right to audit directly the information on service and compensation reported to them by clients. As was suggested also, however, the companies do attempt to make rough liability checks on doubtful situations either under conventional group annuity or deposit administration contracts. Hence, the control function is still exercised but on a less direct basis.

While most companies will write all of the broad classes of contract forms common to the pension field, as well as various combinations of them,[1] some companies, either out of policy or out of circumstance, seem to specialize in particular arrangements. Thus one company known to the writer appears to give most emphasis to its deposit administration contracts. Another concentrates its promotional efforts on split-funding arrangements with a group permanent feature in most of them. Still another emphasizes individual policy plans for smaller employers. There are, of course, limits set by customer preferences to this sort of specialization, and these preferences to the extent that they are essentially uniform among customers tend to blur the differences among insurance carriers.

It is quite clear that competition among insurance companies, as well as among insurance companies and other funding agencies, tends to be complex because of the likely differential impact of the different contract forms upon the needs and desires of clients. While charges to the client are uniformly quoted in terms of annuity purchase rates, reflecting mortality assumptions, interest accretions, and charges for expenses and contingencies, the products sold

---

[1] Cf. Dan M. McGill, *Fundamentals of Private Pensions* (Homewood, Ill.: Richard D. Irwin, Inc., 1955), chap. 3.

and the charges differ in terms of guarantees and/or benefits, as is well known. Also of course the charges have to be considered as a whole and in the context of a time dimension, so that there may be further complications. More will be said about this complexity below in the discussion of competition.

One seemingly important effect of the differences in promotional efforts among insurance companies is the impact on their internal organizations. The traditional basis of departmentation in the insurance company seems to be highly functional. That is to say, the major departments are sales, actuary, investment, administration, legal, and controller's. The different products offered by the insurance company are handled in their several aspects by the respective functional departments, with necessary co-ordination being via interdepartmental committees and also through top-management resolution. Sales are often subdivided into product categories, such as group and ordinary life.

Now, however, it appears that many companies, to expedite their operations in the pension field, have set up special departments for this purpose. Combined under one head for activity in the pension field will be sales, actuary, and administrative, as well as some special service personnel. The point of this seems to be greater ease of maneuver, especially in the matter of meeting requests from clients for combination plans. Presumably with such an arrangement there will be greater ease in convening three of the key functional activities. Significantly it appears that top-management supervision is customarily somewhat less with this type of product departmentation and that the influence of the company's selling agents is greater.

Bank Operations

Banks undoubtedly were originally custodians of funds. However, it seems quite natural that other functions would become less vestigial. With their entrance into the pension field the banks also became investment managers, record keepers, disbursers of pension monies, and, in line with their fiduciary responsibilities, guardians of the funds in such matters as keeping track of the demise of pensioners. Also some banks apparently attempt to supervise the adequacy of the funds in their pension plans, and all seem to watch this.

Policies vary among banks with respect to the performance of many of these functions. As was just intimated some banks feel responsible for what they believe to be the financial soundness of the pension plans which they handle. Others do not, taking the position that their responsibility is confined to the handling of the money.

The detail in which records are kept also seems to vary as a matter of policy and, quite probably, economics. Some banks apparently keep fairly complete records on the covered employees in certain of their pension plans, presumably at the instance of the sponsoring employers. Other banks, out of fiduciary considerations, will keep separate employee records in the case of employee contributions made in contributory pension plans and only summary records on the employer's contribution. Still other banks will have nothing to do with record keeping other than the totals of payments to the fund. On the matter of disbursements to pensioners there appear to be banks which insist on having this function run through them. As has been suggested in Chapter III, many employers have persuaded their banks (and insurance companies) to allow the employer to disburse at least the initial pension payment.

In the management of investments the policy of some banks is apparently strictly against sharing this with a third party, whether it be an employer, an investment counselor, or another bank, as would be necessary with a multiple-trustee arrangement. On the other hand, many banks accept joint-management status and, in the case of competent third parties, apparently are not unhappy about it. More will be said about this matter below.

Just as insurance companies often tend to emphasize some part of the market, banks in the pension field are oriented in "wholesale," "retail," and both directions. A "wholesale" bank in the pension field is one which deals exclusively in larger plans—fifty covered members was given by one wholesale source as the minimum size plan which will be taken on. "Retail" banks will deal with smaller plans and have worked out such arrangements as common trust funds presumably for this purpose.

It will be noted that the banks tend not to give as full service in the pension field as the insurance companies, who are prepared to design plans and provide other services to the client. This difference may be illusory since there is considerable evidence of the existence of informal arrangements between banks and service agencies, such as actuaries and consultants, for the purpose of providing fuller service. This will be discussed in more detail in the next chapter.

Also, lest the ability of the bank to cater to "one-stop shopping" desires of customers be underestimated, it is to be remembered that the banks perform other services for their clients. The most notable are those which are sometimes described as normal banking service. In addition, some banks apparently provide consulting services, on such questions as business expansion, to their pension clients. This is done with the aid of personnel in the bank's industrial loan department which has to be concerned with questions of this sort.

Bank fee arrangements are somewhat complex, though perhaps not quite so much as those of insurance companies which have to quote, among other things, annuity prices. The larger banks have separate fee schedules for custodial work alone and for combined custodial and investment work, both graduated so that the percentage charge declines with the size of the fund. Although the differences between these two fee schedules is usually not great, smaller banks often have one schedule of fees, whether or not their work is purely custodial or custodial and investment management. These smaller banks appear to take their fee schedules more seriously also. The larger banks often negotiate with the client when large sums of money are involved. Quite probably these practices reflect the competitive circumstances in which the bank find themselves.

In addition to fees for custodial and investment management service, it is customary for banks to make additional charges for extra administrative work such as detailed record keeping, if they do this work, and for issuing checks. Some banks also claim that they levy a charge for "wash sales" of securities done at the behest of the sponsoring employer who presumably wants to take his profits. All of these fees and charges are usually paid by the employer rather than by the fund in the case of single-employer plans. The banks having a "wash sale" fee require that the employer pay this.

Bank organization, too, has been somewhat affected by the special character of pension business. Organizationally the business development officer, trust administration, and trust investment have in the past been parallel organization entities working under the supervision of the trust committee of the bank, the later made up of high officers and directors. Now, however, presumably because of the distinctiveness of pension trust activities as compared with other types of trust work, pension departments are getting, either formally or informally, their own investment and in some cases administrative sections working under the immediate supervision of the senior pension executive. There has seemingly been no diminution of top-management control. However, the flow of information and authority within many banks has become more direct.

Some of the smaller banks which have been active competitors for pension business have turned over development, investment, and administrative phases to one man and apparently have also relaxed top-level supervision of the pension executive. These are rather close-knit situations, however, and the difference in top-level supervision may well be less than appears on the surface.

The mode of operation of small banks in the pension field is also quite different than that of larger operators, as might be expected. Smaller banks doing a smaller volume of pension business are in a position to (and have to for economic reasons) dispense with a number of the usual intermediaries found in large-bank operations, especially investment analysts. They substitute for these the time and resources of the executive who in the best of circumstances can bring special attention and ideas to the investment of particular pension funds. The pension executives of larger banks with larger volumes of pension business perforce have to work through subordinates, for whom they will prepare programs of action, including idealized investment lists, etc. The larger bank obviously has an advantage in the diversity of opinion which can be brought to bear on such crucial matters as investment but a disadvantage in having to oversee the action of a considerable number of junior subordinates. The smaller bank does not have the latter problem, but its pension executive has to compensate in some way for the lack of advisory resources within his organization.

Investment Counselors and Mutual Funds

In dealing with the operations of investment counselors and mutual funds the distinction between types of business handled by the various operators in the field is of paramount importance. There is first the operator who might be described as the "old-line" investment counselor who is unassociated with other agencies and who performs functions which are purely advisory. A second, smaller category uncovered in the present investigation is the investment counselor who works in association with an actuary. A third and perhaps increasingly important variety of investment counselor is one who works for a mutual fund and who advises the fund, its salesmen (who may also receive actuarial advice and service from the fund actuary in connection with selling pension plans), and clients who do not choose to buy shares of the mutual fund.

While all three of these types of investment counselors perform the functions of drawing up investment policy recommendations, the auspices under which this operation takes place differ, as can be seen. Also the nature and emphasis in the additional functions which they perform seems to differ. The unassociated advisor will be advising the client company directly on the general question of investment policy. He will also be making suggestions to the client and possibly to the client's corporate trustee regarding current operations of the fund. Finally he will be in communication with the client's actuary regarding the proper interest rate assumptions and the payout projection from the fund; the latter so that there can be a proper matching of maturities of liabilities and investments. It is of more than passing interest that apparently the latter subject, which is important in balancing the portfolio, is not in all cases well handled. That is to say, some counselors complain about not being able to get a payout projection.

The advisor who is associated in practice with an actuary is likely to be helping the actuary make his evaluation of the different funding agencies, so that the actuary may make his report containing this material to his client. On occasion also the investment counselor will at the request of the actuary review the portfolio activities of the bank trustee and possibly make suggestions for changes through the actuary.

Aside from the other duties mentioned above, the investment counselor working for the mutual fund will presumably develop a portfolio policy recommendation for his clients who do not buy shares of the mutual fund and advise them on current operations. It appears to be true at the present time that the work of this type of investment counselor is not as closely integrated with the work of the client's actuary as that of the other two kinds of investment counselors. But this may change as the mutual funds develop actuarial departments or affiliations with actuarial firms, and they apparently are beginning to do this.

There are some investment funds which are operated essentially for the convenience of the old-line investment counselor. These may increase if the role of this type of investment counselor should increase in the pension field, since they tend to be preferred by him. They are likely to lay heavy emphasis on growth stocks which seem to be preferred at the present time by investment counselors working in the pension field. The advantage to the investment counselor gained from putting his clients into such a fund is said to be the great latitude achieved in portfolio management. The fund managers may within legal limits handle investments according to their own inclinations once the client has bought his shares.

The "open-end" mutual fund to which the third type of investment counselor mentioned is associated is, however, an end in itself, and this, rather than the associated investment counseling service, is the main object of sales activity. To this end such funds have marketing organizations and affiliated agents whose personnel are probably more numerous than the number of personnel performing the portfolio management and other activities taken on by the fund.

Fees and charges made to the client reflect the purposes and working relationships discussed. The old-line investment counselor is likely to charge the client a percentage of the fund handled, or a flat fee, and also to get adjustment upwards of his fee with good performance. The actuary-associated investment counselor is presumably compensated by the actuary for services rendered. Investment advisors employed by mutual funds are likely to charge a fee based on the size of the fund of the client who does not elect to buy the shares of the fund. If he does so elect the client may pay nothing directly except the "loading" charge on fund shares. The investment advisor is compensated through a management fee levied directly on the mutual fund.

The organization and size of investment counseling operations are also reflective of the types of operation mentioned above. The counselor working for the actuary is likely to be a one-man operation. The unassociated counselor may well be a somewhat larger operation, since he is likely to be counseling other clients besides pension clients. If this is the case, he will employ two types of personnel—principals who will together formulate investment policy and individually deal with clients, investment researchers, and analysts, and of course clerical staff. The investment counseling organization working for the mutual fund is likely to be quite large because of its varied duties. Its staff will include researchers, "account executives," and business developers, as well as the executive group which sets investment policy. These personnel are likely to be working on other business besides that of pension clients, although apparently there in some division of labor.

Competition among Funding Agents and Financial Advisors

As has been suggested already competition on a price basis within and among the various funding media is a complicated business in view of the diverse methods of charging and in view of the sometimes considerable differences in the products offered. The sales developers of all of the funding agencies have gone to great lengths to develop meaningful (and sometimes unfortunately not so meaningful) cost comparisons of the different arrangements which might be made when a private pension plan is to be funded. Most of these treatises on costs are probably not generally comprehensive, however.

Larger clients usually have the resources to make careful investigations. The writer has seen some extremely well-done analyses of costs and other factors relevant to the choice of a funding medium and agency.[2] Hence the choices of larger clients are likely to be much better-informed

---

[2] Unfortunately he may not use these analyses here.

choices, although, of course, not necessarily better choices, in view of the uncertainty connected with making many relevant estimates and in view of the fact that other things besides measurable data determine the quality of the choice.

As in other market situations where price competition is not the only dimension of competition (or not important), sellers attempt to establish themselves with their clients by other means. Accusations or undue and unfair influence by competitors in the funding field were made by practically every funding agency representative the writer interviewed. Except for certain instances to be alluded to later in this section, the writer does not feel qualified to pass judgment on such charges. However, it does appear that prior connections which the funding agency may have with the client or with key client executives and, to some extent, key advisors do often provide the push which turns the pension business to a particular funding agency.[3]

This is not to underestimate the effectiveness of the considerable amount of sales development work carried on by insurance agents, mutual fund salesmen, and, on perhaps a more restrained level, by bank and investment counsel development people. Judging by the efforts put into sales aids for some of these people, the results must not be insignificant and are probably quite effective with smaller clients.

Nor should we overlook in discussing this matter of undue influence the care with which many large firms approach their choice of a funding agency or combination. Some of these firms make a particular effort to distribute their pension and other funds among the agencies which are interested in having them, although, as will be discussed in a moment, these firms apparently have other reasons for

---

[3] Cf. Chapter II; also Chapter VII.

some of the distributions which they have made of their pension money.

Most of the funding agencies compete with each other. In the case of insurance companies engaged in direct selling, as well as selling through agents, and also in the case of the mutual fund investment counseling combinations, which were discussed previously, there is competition within a particular funding agency. Whether or not all of this competition is desirable in view of the differences of some of the products and their suitability to all classes of customers is of course a question which has been hotly debated. It evidently bothers some of the more candid funding agency representatives talked to. These people feel that only "consumer education" will prevent client mistakes made under the pressure of competition.

Despite the market-wide competition which takes place, however, there appear to be tendencies towards segmentation of the market for competitive purposes, as has been indicated already in the earlier discussion. Broadly speaking some insurance companies, the wholesale banks, and, to an increasing extent as far as investment advice is concerned, the old-line investment counselors appear to compete hardest for the pension business of the larger clients. The most vigorous competition for smaller clients seems to be among insurance companies with special-plans departments, retail banks, and, increasingly, the mutual funds.

While no comprehensive data are available, there appears to have been a growth of combination plans which involve working relationships between insurance companies and banks, as well as combinations involving several banks. The latter type of combination is embodied in the multiple-trustee arrangement negotiated by some large industrial concerns. From the internal memoranda which the writer has seen, the chief motivation of the client here appears to be the diversification of investments which it is believed will be obtained by distributing the pension monies to several banks situated in different parts of the country and presumably familiar with different parts of the business economy. Also, as has been suggested, there apparently is some idea of a "fair distribution" of funds, a motive which would be worth discussing further from the standpoint of pension security were it not so evidently subordinated to diversification and were not the list of qualified bank bidders so exclusive.

The use of both an insurance company and a bank in the servicing of pension clients has of course taken place to some extent in the past. However, the notable recent development here has been the split-funding arrangement whereby the client (and his employees, in the case of contributory plans) allocates pension money both to the insurance company directly and to the banks, who will accumulate a fund to be used eventually for the purchase of annuities. The client interest here was originally to take advantage of the "third-party guarantee" of certain insurance company contracts and at the same time participate in substantial common stock investments by bank trustees. More recently clients seem to be interested in split-funding in order to obtain a different kind of diversification of investment.

Some operators in both the insurance and the banking fields apparently find the split-funding arrangement very acceptable under current competitive circumstances (although probably for different reasons). Nonetheless, there is concern in both groups on the ground that with certain types of split-funding it is somewhat more difficult for either the bank or the insurance company to keep a check on the client's funding behavior since in some instances neither agency knows for sure how much money is allocated to the other. This criticism, while it suggests serious possibilities from the standpoint of pension security, is probably to be softened somewhat by the fact that it applies to the plans of larger clients who are accustomed to taking more complete responsibility in the management of their pension affairs. It is customary (and obviously desirable) in such instances to have an independent actuary who serves co-ordinative functions and evaluates the sufficiency of the fund.

In this discussion of the character of competition among the funding agencies a final note should be made of the changes or attempts to change and expand the type of services offered to the client. The effect of these changes, which have taken a somewhat similar pattern in the case of the service agencies discussed in the next chapters, has tended to make the different types of funding agencies more similar with respect to their offerings to the prospective client. The development of deposit administration and immediate participation guarantee contracts by insurance companies and common trust funds for smaller pension clients by the banks are realities in this respect. We should mention also the partially successful attempts of insurance companies in getting permission from state legislatures to establish separate common stock funds for pension business, as well as the attempts by some banks and mutual funds to get "supertrust" powers as a means of averaging the experience risks associated with smaller pension plans. These latter developments and ideas are perhaps even clearer indications of an important dimension of competition in this part of the pension field.

The Impact of Competition: Insurance Companies

The vigorous competitive climate among funding agencies as well as the demand discussed in Chapter IV for more discretion by many clients could be expected to result in numerous pressures on and judgmental situations for the several funding agencies. As was suggested at the end of the earlier discussion, financial management by clients, the way in which such pressures have been handled and the judgmental situations resolved has a good deal of significance for the question of pension security. As we know these things have been important topics in previous discussions of the private pension field. Hence a particular point was made in the present investigation to inquire into such pressures and judgments as one might expect to come up.

We have already noted the development of the deposit administration contract as a competitive instrument by insurance companies and the problems seen by the insurance industry to be associated with the options frequently given in such contracts. As has also been suggested, the problem of controlling client funding and administrative behavior under deposit administration can be overemphasized in view of the indirect checks which are frequently possible.

In addition, the insurance representatives talked with uniformly noted that the scaling down of the insurance company's individual pension guarantee in the case of the unallocated active life deposit administration fund was not a significant change from their point of view since the reputation of the company with the public is involved with any pension arrangement in which it participates. And it was noted that some state regulatory bodies would make inquiry of the insurance company in the event of an employer default, regardless of the liability of the insurance company under its contract with the employer.

One consultant interviewed offered what might be a useful summary opinion here by suggesting that the only occasion to worry about deposit administration contracts is in the case of certain negotiated plans where, as was discussed earlier in this book, there may have been too much emphasis on "cents per hour" and too little on the associated benefits promised. Less protection is offered against the excesses of collective bargaining by this type of contract than comes with other types of insurance company contracts which are somewhat more formal in their insistence on adequate financial provision. When cents per hour has not been the only thing thought about in setting up a pension plan, however, this problem is not as likely to be acute, from the standpoint of pension security, as the discussion of the previous paragraph suggests.

A particular topic of interest in this discussion of the impact of competition in the pension field on insurance companies is the multidimensional price competition within the insurance industry and between the industry and other agencies. The writer has taken note of a certain amount of what he would call "misleading advertising" on the extent of interest guarantees and their significance to pension costs especially. This kind of promotional activity seems to be concentrated in the plans of a few companies and is definitely considered "beyond the pale" by most of the big insurance operators within the pension field. It is, nevertheless, a rather serious problem from the standpoint of pension security, in view of the bearing which things like interests rates have on the construction of a financial plan for a pension arrangement. While obscuring the extent of interest guarantees will fool no qualified professional in the pension field, the client himself is likely to have a hand in the choice of a funding agency, and, by virtue of the organization of the pension industry, he may not have a qualified professional to advise him.

The adoption of "new money" policies for investment

income allocation within insurance companies has been another result in a sense of competition among the several types of funding agencies, although conditions internal to the insurance industry seem to have had an influence, too. As is well known, this change works out at the present time in favor of the pension business of an insurance company since pension contributions have been heavy during the recent period of rising interest rates. Probably the only observation which needs to be made here is that if the money market ever gets into a long softening stage and hence into a period of declining interest rates, the liberal longer-term guarantees of interest accretion which seem to have been developed for pension clients under the influence of this change in investment income allocation policy, as well as under the influence of tight money conditions currently prevailing, could be embarrassing to the insurance companies offering the liberal guarantees.[4]

A final point inquired into of the insurance companies in view of the competitiveness of the pension field and the current inclinations of many clients to weave pensions into over-all financial affairs was that of the response of the insurance companies to requests for loans from clients. Some companies in their promotional literature for pensions mention the availability of loans to clients and others do this in a way which implies preferential treatment. There was no evidence uncovered that such statements really mean anything in practice. This finding seems reasonable in view of the seemingly great separation as far as influence is concerned between the investment group of the typical insurance company and its other departments, regardless of the

---

[4] The New York State Insurance Department in a recent ruling apparently has banned "new money" status. Cf. *National Life Underwriter*, December 17, 1960.

type of organization of these. Also of course one supposes that regulatory bodies would make special inquiry into this kind of practice of reciprocation.

The Impact of Competition: Banks

In the earlier discussion of bank operations and competition the point was made that some banks evidently do and others do not apply pressure on their clients in the matter of the adequacy and general state of the client's pension fund. The variation in practice here seemed less associated with competitive forces and positions than with differences in points of view as to what bank prerogatives are in the case of noninvestment aspects of pension plans. It is perhaps of some significance here that the bankers who told the interviewer that advising the client on other than investment matters was none of their business uniformly also indicated that they tried to keep up on the client's affairs, including his pension affairs, by a variety of means—in the case of pensions by getting hold of actuarial reports. In the case of new business some banks apparently check into the credit rating of the pension client, while the top managements of others enjoin their pension development people to exercise extreme care on the choice of clients. On some occasions the bank may request appointment as "custodian" rather than as "trustee."

A great deal was said also in the earlier discussion of financial management activities by clients in the matter of client's policy-making role and review processes, as well as the day-to-day contacts, carried on with the banks. As was pointed out, the day-to-day contacts were seemingly encouraged by the banks in order to maintain their position with the client. They also, however, occasionally seem to lead to requests from the client which the bank considers inappropriate.

The banks appear to have given a great deal of thought to policies and tactics aimed at parrying such thrusts and appear to be successful much of the time. Investments in the client's securities or notes are an example of this, and if the bank agrees to this at all it will usually be on an insured-loan basis.

Pension officers of the large banks with important pension business appear generally to be under rather explicit instructions from the top management of their banks regarding many types of investment and financial accommodations involving the client's pension fund. Because of this and because the pension officer is undoubtedly judged in part by the volume of business done by his department, he is obviously therefore under pressure to use his powers of persuasion with the client who makes direct requests for many of the kinds of accommodation discussed earlier in this report.

As concerns the review processes which are carried on by many larger clients, the impact may actually be greater because of the psychological pressure brought to bear, especially when the bank is a member of a multiple-trustee arrangement. In one such multiple-trustee case the representative, after impressing upon the writer the competitiveness of the situation (which happened not to be true in terms of the wishes of the sponsoring client) went on to say that he was getting a little dubious about the value of diversified portfolios. He was responding to his view of the arrangements, including the motives behind the review process being conducted by the client.

Some banks apparently have refused to let themselves

get into the situation where the client may make an exhaustive and detailed review, presumably because of doubts about the purpose and wisdom of clients' review processes. This type of pressure imposed by the client, in light of the competitiveness of the pension field, may be worth further study in terms of its effects on desirable portfolio management.

One other result of bank competitive measures taken in the pension field deserves some attention. This is the use of the idealized investment list and its formal counterpart, the common trust fund, by banks which have come to service very large numbers of clients, many of them small. There is an obvious administrative convenience from such arrangements and probably a great deal to be said for them from the standpoint of pension security, since the programing is likely to be done by the ablest people on the bank's staff. However, the question of applicability to different pension situations is to be raised. Some of these situations, for example, because of varying payout expectations may have different liquidity and maturity requirements. If these are not taken into consideration, losses may be taken or gains foregone or costs entailed through the borrowing of necessary cash. To what extent the "management by exception" principle has been developed and applied in conjunction with the use of idealized lists and common trusts was not ascertained. Such a practice seems a necessity when investment management is carried on by the devices under discussion.

The Impact of Competition: Mutual Funds

The impact of competition in the pension field and of client financial inclinations is harder to discuss in the case of mutual funds. This is partly because to an extent their arrival is probably to be attributed to the competitive situation which has been described. As of the present, however, there are some indications that many of the funds have not been at pains to clarify the comparative cost picture between themselves and competing media and agencies. Whether clients have been misled is, of course, something which depends upon performance of the funds taken in conjunction with all relevant charges, and we do not have these data.

Similarly the question of applicability of the portfolio of a mutual fund to the needs of pension client shareholders with varying payout schedules has to be raised here, too, especially if the portfolio emphasizes to any degree speculative common stocks. There are, of course, balanced mutual funds whose fluctuations in value are relatively small. Some of the funds also apparently are developing combination arrangements with insurance companies to provide additional investment diversification and stability for pension clients. Finally, a number of mutual funds are either developing their own actuarial departments or are affiliating with agencies having actuarial personnel in them. Conceivably these steps will eventually give better co-ordination with the needs of pension plans than exists at the present time.

Security Aspects of Funding Agencies: Summary

It is quite clear that neither employers with particular financial inclinations regarding the management of their pension activities nor the funding agencies servicing pension clients are operating in a vacuum with respect to each other and therefore have things pretty much as they wish. The funding agencies have quite obviously had to adapt, in terms of products offered, functions performed, and quite possibly peace of mind vis à vis many of their clients. On the other hand, this adaptation has manifestly not been a surrender, such that pension security has become completely vulnerable to some of the possibly less desirable manifestations of client financial initiative. This latter fact is clearly indicated by the evidence of continuing concern on the part of insurance companies and many banks with the question of the adequacy of the client's fund, as well as by the policy postures evidently taken and the tactical maneuvers worked out by these agencies to deal with questionable requests.

There have been some unfortunate consequences of the competitive climate. One is the obscuration of the true outlay costs associated with using the different funding arrangements. Another is the apparent psychological impact of competition on some of the funding agencies. This conceivably could bring difficulties from a security point of view. Another is undoubtedly in the poor choice of a funding vehicle and/or plan made by some clients under the pressure of the sales personnel of some funding agencies and given the wide range of choice now available.

Something, of course, is to be said for this range of choice in that it provides the client with some bargaining power. Also the development of new funding choices which has been taking place in the pension field has quite probably brought arrangements which are more suitable to the needs of some plans, from every point of view, than have been the more limited choices available in the past.

Chapter VII

CONSULTANTS, ACTUARIES, AND INDEPENDENT ADMINISTRATORS

The Development of Pension Service Agencies

The pension service agencies—consultants, actuaries, and independent administrators—like the funding agencies have gone through stages of development. Most of the older agencies have at one time or another apparently been associated with the insurance industry, as brokers or in a service affiliation. More recently many of these have disassociated themselves and have even in varying degrees taken on informal affiliations with other funding agencies. The reverse seems to have happened too.

Another change which appears to have taken place is that many of these older agencies started out operating on a rather general advisory basis in pension and related fields. Subsequently, some of them developed into specialists, especially in the actuarial field, retaining only for older customers some of the other services once a part of the "product line." The specialist agencies, as might be expected, are usually attached on a consulting basis to very large clients.

Still others of the older group of agencies appear to have maintained the breadth of their offerings but have hired specialists to handle various functions. It would appear that this latter group of agencies tends to service medium- and smaller-sized business, as well as unions and multiple-employer plans. In the latter instance it has been noted in Chapter V that the outside agency is likely to be performing a rather large set of functions.

At some relatively late stage of the development of service agencies in the pension field, the independent administrator appears to have come into existence. Partly this seems to have been due to some special problems and economic situations arising in the pension field, as will be discussed. Partly the development is to be accounted for by a disinclination on the part of many consultants and actuaries to do certain rather routine types of work. In some respects the "pendulum" here seems to be swinging back in the other direction, however.

Operations of Pension Consultants

Typically the modern independent pension consultant is primarily concerned with three activities for his client. The first of these is working out the basic features of the client's pension plan in consideration of the client's objectives, situation, and preferences. As has been noted earlier, this work involves working rather closely with the highest authorities in the client firm or with the trustee board of a multiple-employer plan. The same is true in connection with the second primary function of the consultant, which is to make an analysis of alternative funding arrangements to help the client in his decision. This function is sometimes a perfunctory one if the preferences of the client are strongly in favor of a particular agency or if the consultant is brought in by a funding agency.

A third primary function of the pension consultant is to set up the systems and procedures which will be necessary for the effective and efficient operation of the pension plan. The chief subjects here involve, first, taking care that the proper records are kept on employee age, sex, service, and, if the plan requires, compensation and contributions of employees; and, second, working out the proper flow and schedule for information required for actuarial work, benefit administration, internal reports, for example, to the company management, and for external reports to the various government agencies which require filings related to pension activities.

In addition to these primary activities pension consultants not infrequently perform certain other services. One of these is the actuarial estimation of liabilities and assets necessary to the structuring of the plan and the periodic reviews necessary after the plan has gotten under way for purposes of internal and external review. The latter is carried on by the client's public accountants and, in certain cases, by union pension experts and public agencies.

Another service is assisting in the filing of information for Internal Revenue certification, as well as the reports required under the various federal and state disclosure laws. A third is the preparation of informational literature and procedures for the client's covered employees. Finally, but less frequently, the consultant may do the actual record keeping and benefit administration for the client. The renaissance alluded to in this area seems to have taken the form of the consultant having an affiliated or subsidiary data-processing firm handle the records of clients.

It is less frequent for the pension consultant to prepare the various legal documents describing and implementing the client's pension plan. However, some do, using the argument that the client's counsel is unable or disinterested in carrying through on these functions. In relatively rare instances the consultant will perform certain personnel functions associated with pensions, such as informing an exiting employee of any pension rights which he might have under his employer's plan and advising him what to do in such cases where there are options. Not so infrequent, apparently, is the participation of the independent consultant in collective bargaining carried on by his client. The consultant technically is never in the formal status of a negotiator. Nonetheless, it seems to happen that he is on occasion negotiating the pension sections of the collective bargaining discussion with a consultant or actuary working for the union.

If the consultant is employed by a union on a consulting or a full-time basis he will do work on plan characteristics for collective bargaining purposes. Also, in such cases where the union may have some administrative functions, he will work on administrative procedures to be carried out by shop stewards and other union personnel. And he will participate on the same basis as employer consultants in collective bargaining. In addition the union consultant may perform various other tasks, especially those which come up when plans are fully or partially terminated for reasons of plant shutdown, merger, etc. In such instances the consultant may end up as a trustee of what remains.

In the case of multiple-employer plans it was noted earlier that the consultant frequently performs the role of general advisor and, among other things, helps on financial decisions. Finally, some consultants still operate also as brokers and are compensated for this.

In view of the variations in consultant functions just enumerated one finds great differences in the size of consulting firms. The three primary functions can be performed by an individual working alone and very often are. At the other extreme of the size class are the agencies which will

have a considerable number of personnel employed or affiliated and which are likely to be performing more than the
three primary functions. In such instances the work force
is likely to include "outside men," developing business and
working with clients, "inside" personnel, the specialists
needed to perform the various functions handled by the
agency, and, in addition, the usual clerical and stenographic
people. Charges for consultant service, as with most pension
service agencies, are apparently always on a classified-time
basis, except perhaps for the preliminary study, which is
done either free, as part of the sales procedure, or more
usually on a flat-fee basis. The reason given for these particular fee arrangements was that most of the operations
performed are of unpredictable time-length and difficulty.

Operations of Actuaries

In theory the work of the actuary might seem to begin
after the "spade work" on a pension plan has taken place
and when preliminary estimates of liabilities and assets
pertinent to proposed features of the pension plan are required. The division of labor is frequently not so drawn,
however, and the actuary is often in the picture at the beginning, helping design the plan, providing information on
funding agencies, and setting up data systems and procedures. From a co-ordination standpoint there are many
desirable features to this frequent early participation by
the actuary.

After the pension plan is in operation the work of the
professional actuary takes place on a periodic basis, usually
once a year. He prepares reports on the liability of the plan.
In connection with this work he takes note of developing
experience and on this basis may recommend changes of
assumptions made in previous valuations. The items usually

involved here will be turnover, mortality, interest on and appreciation of the investment assets of the plan, and, if they are relevant, compensation levels and expenses of retirement and of disability.

As is the case when the work is done by a consultant working as an actuary, these periodic reports are used in various internal and external reviews of the pension plan. It might be added here, in line with the remarks made in the discussion of financial management by clients, that the actuary's reports should be of considerable importance to certain actions taken in this area, including a change in the contribution of a firm to its plan.

Another periodic function of the actuary is to make forecasts of the payouts from the fund which the client might be accumulating either with an insurance company under a deposit administration arrangement or with a bank trustee. These forecasts have relevance to any funding agency estimate of the adequacy of the client's fund and also, in the case of most bank-trusteed plans, to the liquidity requirements of the portfolio, as has been indicated previously. It is charged by some of the funding agencies and investment advisors that the forecasts are apparently often not made, or, if they are made, not transmitted to these agencies. In some cases, it is said by actuaries that employers will not pay for such payment projections. In other cases such projections are said to be discouraged since increased liquidity usually leads to lower investment earnings.

At the very least all this suggests an area of communications which needs to be improved. A sterner view would be that ultimate objectives are being disregarded.

In addition to these activities the independent actuary will sometimes be in a supervising or senior position with respect to other actuaries retained on a local basis by multilocation forms. Sometimes, too, an actuary is called in periodically to review the work of another actuary. He will also do, on occasion, the other activities listed above as done by the consultant. Hence, the distinction between the two types of agencies is sometimes difficult to make in practice. In general, however, actuaries being specialists tend to perform these other functions less frequently than consultants. When the actuarial agency is more than a one-man operation, this tendency of performing other functions, too, is reflected in a higher percentage of nonactuarial personnel. Also, as has been noted at various places earlier in this report, many actuarial agencies have affiliations with other types of service agencies for their own convenience and for the convenience of their clients.

Operations of Independent Administrators

The primary functions of those agencies which classify themselves as independent administrators appear to be in the record keeping and processing area. These agencies usually include as their clients multiple-employer plans and smaller single-employer plans. On occasion, economic considerations connected with data processing, as well as the inclinations of the employer concerning record keeping and data processing, result in independent administrators handling medium- and larger-sized plans.

To function properly in record keeping and in the preparation of reports for benefit administration, actuarial work, and various other internal and external reviews where data on employee service and/or compensation are required, the independent administrator must of course have access to original personnel and subsequent service records. The early development of the agency in the pension field has been apparently due to the difficulties of obtaining such information. In some cases, employers, usually smaller ones, were not accustomed to keeping such records and hence had to be instructed and supervised in doing so. This became perhaps the earliest area for the administrator, presumably out of a disinclination of more generalized pension consultants to take on the work.

Then came the growth of union funds and later multiple-employer plans of the Taft-Hartley variety, which were contributed to on a service and/or compensation basis by the employers who had contracted to do so. At this point the obtaining of essential service and payroll records presumably became more complex and difficult because of the number of participants and the differences among them. Also, in certain fields such as construction, where employers frequently operate on a transient basis, the problem of keeping up with employment activity covered by the multiple-employer plan became a real one, calling for the skills of a detective. Apparently some union business agents were disinclined or unable to handle the problem of seeing that contributions to the fund were made by the transient employer coming into the area covered by the fund. The provision for and doing of this detective work became one of the functions of independent administrators in fields like construction.

Quite possibly the independent administrator is now realizing an additional advantage and getting additional business as the result of the economies of large-scale data processing. This was said to be the case by some of the administrators interviewed. However, no data were obtained on this development.

Besides handling the work of record keeping and processing as described above some administrators also set up records systems for clients and provide reports on pension accumulations to employees of clients who buy the record keeping and processing service and who desire that this sort of information be dispensed, as increasingly seems to be the case. Both of these services are obvious by-products of the primary service of record keeping.

Actuarial work is not done typically by the administrator. However, many do advise on the structure of pension plans, especially for smaller clients. To the extent that actuarial service needs to be provided, the independent administrator will either retain or maintain an affiliation with an actuary.

The Nature of Competition

Most consultants, actuaries, and independent administrators tend to compete with each other by virtue of the variety of often similar services performed by each agency. The number of competitors is, however, somewhat smaller than the total number of the three types of agencies because of the affiliations and tie-ins which have been mentioned above.

In addition, the market tends to be segmented into an employer section and a union section. That is to say, most of the agencies which have been discussed above specialize either in consulting for employers or for unions but not for both, the one exception being Taft-Hartley plans which have apparently attracted some employer-oriented actuaries in view of the frequent practice of having only one actuarial consultant for such plans. Aside from this exception, the segmentation which is believed by the trade to be required has an unfortunate connotation from the standpoint of pension security, since in a sense a conflict would appear to be thereby "built in" to negotiations on subjects which affect the security of promised benefits. Some consultants argued that it is desirable to have two competent consultants looking at a case from different points of view since there are so many unresolved areas, especially in the actuarial field. More will be said about this subject below.

New business is to a large extent obtained by consultants, actuaries, and independent administrators on a referral basis. Some business is, however, obtained directly by various methods, including some direct selling. The referrals to a given agency or group of affiliates come very often from a particular type of funding agency, rather than from all types. This segmentation, too, raises questions. It should be noted, however, that many of the service agencies have in the past shifted their funding agency relationships and presumably would do so in the future if they thought that they should.

After a client is obtained initially, the chief means of retention appears to be that of service offered the client. Variety of services is apparently a factor with clients. However, accessibility of the client to a principal in the service agency and frequent service calls by this principal are more important. An interesting note on the success of business retention by the pension service agencies is the fact that nearly all of the employers interviewed were using their original service agencies. Changes seem to be usual only as the result of mergers of client companies.

Nature and Significance of Disagreements

A natural topic of discussion concerning the service-agency field from the standpoint of pension security is the specialization of service affiliations into union-management and funding agency categories. Disagreements exist among these variously affiliated consultants and actuaries and they involve essentially questions of policy on funding rather than basic data and actuarial assumptions. This is not to say that there are not differences in practice in treating these latter items.[1]

As has been noted in the discussions of Chapters IV and VI the two subjects of rate of funding and choice of funding medium are very difficult ones. An intelligent decision on them from any point of view involves a good deal more than actuarial estimates of the amount of money required to provide pensions. The rate of funding is also related to client financial policy and position, the funding medium to the different objectives which might be appropriate for different pension situations. These subjects are in a very great sense not actuarial in their primary aspects, although the actuary by virtue of his practical experience and knowledge is likely to be in an excellent position to comment and is frequently called upon to do so.

In view of the lack of operational standards for dealing with these very complex questions of policy, the only thing that seems fair to discuss from the standpoint of pension security is whether or not independent actuaries, insofar as can be observed, make a clear distinction to the client as between their legitimate professional opinions and their personal preferences. This is a very difficult inquiry to make because of its inherent subtleties. Some information of seeming relevance, however was obtained in the field investigation.

On the matter of funding any "past service liability" of a pension plan—this is an area in which there can be many views—the actuaries interviewed uniformly appeared to be on the conservative side personally. That is to say, they were disposed to taking care of past service liability at least

---

[1] Cf. George A. Mooney, *Pension and Other Employee Welfare Plans* (State of New York, 1955), tables 130–34.

to the extent encouraged by the federal tax laws, if this was at all possible for the client.[2] Many actuaries (and consultants doing actuarial work) apparently have no qualms about making their preference known to their client as part of their professional opinion. Generally this part of the opinion is rendered persuasively rather than authoritatively, the degree seeming to be tied in with the extent to which the actuary is established in general and with his client. Less frequently the actuary or consultant insists on a definite schedule of past service payments as a condition of servicing the client. One consultant doing considerable actuarial work remarked, in reply to the interviewer's question that the consultant seemed pretty insistent on matters of funding, that he was well enough established that he could afford to be insistent.

On the matter of funding agencies, most actuaries and consultants doing actuarial work, including those with very definite private preferences, said that they made it a policy to give the pros and cons of all major possibilities. An exception usually is taken to this rule in the case of a referral from a funding agency, the rationalization being that the question has already been aired and decided upon. One might remark that certainly in the case of the larger single-employer client, and possibly some multiple-employer plans, the practice of evaluating all funding possibilities is likely to be necessary, since the financial officers usually on hand are knowledgeable enough to ask a lot of questions.

The writer did encounter one investment counselor working for an actuary who said that his (the counselor's) main purpose was to put clients into self-administered plans. It

---

[2] This attitude of actuaries toward past as well as future service liability does not refer to the recognition of these things as a liability of the firm for audit purposes. Cf. Chapter VIII.

was not known how much of his viewpoint went into the actuary's evaluation for his client. However, some probably did.

In summary it would appear that on the matter of funding rate many actuaries and consultants do interject their opinions. It is important to note, however, that they tend to do so in a direction which may not result in the most attractive pension scheme from a current-cost point of view. In the matter of funding agencies, most actuaries and consultants seem a good deal more circumspect about coming out for one in particular. Both of these conclusions and the implications which might be drawn from them, however, have to be regarded as somewhat tentative in view of the nature of the investigative process.

Other Questions Related to Pension Security

By and large the other issues posed by the material presented on the pension service agencies in this section revolve around the question of generalization versus specialization. On the one hand, there is always the question of whether or not an agency offering a diversified line of services, some of them highly specialized, will give proper emphasis to the specialties in its operations.

The opposite question is important too, especially in the pension field, where a great many things have to be coordinated in a way which does not prejudice the proper performance of any of them individually. In this connection, it appeared from the field work that, in spite of the rather substantial degree of integration and affiliation which characterizes the service agencies, there are still problems of coordination to be worked out. One seems to be in the matter of giving more attention to the factor of administerability in working out the characteristics of a pension plan—this was a point made by people engaged primarily in administrative work for pension plans. Another problem appears to be the improvement of communications and understanding between the actuarial and the financial management functions, so that the latter can be conducted more effectively.

Chapter VIII

PUBLIC ACCOUNTANTS AND ATTORNEYS

Introductory Note

Public accountants and attorneys are different from many of the service groups in the pension field in that they have existed for longer than the pension field itself. Their movement into the pension field was obviously necessitated by the growth of the pension movement as an adjunct of business operation and also by the regulation of private pensions. Pension work is handled as just one additional service in the typical accounting or legal firm, as we shall see.

This mode of operation is somewhat similar to the specialist actuary who may be involved in other affairs besides pensions. But it is much more extreme. Also pension matters do not seem to have influenced the basic viewpoints of accountants and lawyers to any great extent. The attitude of the public accountants interviewed was that their primary function was still to protect the stockholders in a firm, nothing more and nothing less. Lawyers in the pension field tend to be neutral about all matters except the quality of the legal documents.

All of this has its advantageous side from the standpoint of the security of pension benefits. In the present context of

law and social forces, good legal work and good accounting
work for the sake of the stockholders probably helps to a
great extent the interests of pensioners and prospective pensioners. However, some problems are likely to come up to the
extent that pension work is carried on by public accountants
and attorneys as something of a sideline. This has tended to
be true until quite recently and has led to some of the issues
which are treated in the following paragraphs.

Functions of Public Accountants

The most frequent and substantial function performed
by public accountants which gets into pension affairs is the
financial audit of the employer with a conventional or negotiated pension plan. It is in the performance of this function
that public accountants are likely to give pension affairs
their most substantial airing since they must, with the aid of
information supplied by the actuary especially, estimate the
firm's liability due to pensions, if there is any. More will be
said about the handling of this problem below.

A second function performed by the public accountant,
and one that is growing more important for reasons which
seem obvious, is the financial audit of the pension fund, if
there is one, and of the whole pension plan in the case of
multiple-employer plans. The most important suboperations
here are the ascertaining of the existence of assets, the valuation of these assets, and the audit of charges to the fund or
plan.

A third function is the summary audit of procedures
used in connection with the collecting and reporting within
the firm or the pension plan of information pertinent to
assets and liabilities of the firm or plan. As far as pensions
are concerned, procedures used to record and report em-

ployees, their service, compensation, etc., as well as the contributions of employers to multiple-employer plans, are of
importance. Some public accountants apparently regard this
summary audit function as a necessary part of the first two
financial audit operations. This seems not to be uniformly
true, however. Also the function is regarded as one requiring
special emphasis and treatment. Hence we treat it separately.

Some public accountants handle for their clients the
filing of plans and subsequent information for tax purposes
with Internal Revenue and, where it is required, the filing of
information on pension liabilities with the Securities and
Exchange Commission. In some cases also they will figure
in the development of the pension plan itself. However, these
functions, particularly the latter, are seemingly performed
much less frequently than the first three.

As is well known, the public accounting firm is typically
a partnership with the partners making policy and reviewing
the accounting work ultimately with the client's board.
Juniors do the "spade work" of collecting information for
the various kinds of audits. Their work, to the extent that it is
not preprogramed, is supervised and reviewed, either by the
partners directly or, in the case of larger public accounting
firms, by semisenior and senior accountants.

There are apparently some variations in the nature as
well as in the comprehensiveness of the instructions given the
juniors, especially in the matter of the auditing of procedures. One difference of relevance to the pension security
subject is the requirement by some, though by no means all,
public accounting firms, that the procedures of interest be
studied in operation and by recourse to the operators rather
than simply by asking higher executives of the enterprise or
plan.

Functions of Lawyers in Pension Work

Lawyers seem usually to function in the pension field as generalists employed in an employer's legal department or by a union or in a general counseling firm retained by an employer. However, there are also some attorneys who are specialists working for some of the large legal firms and for the insurance companies.

The generalist lawyer working for employer, union, or general counsel has as a primary responsibility with respect to pensions the review of the various legal documents prepared in connection with the pension plan. He is also frequently charged with the preparation of these documents and the conduct of negotiations with Internal Revenue for certification of the pension plan, two functions which seem to go together, regardless of who performs them. In this instance the generalist lawyer may rely on model documents, given him by pension consultants, actuaries, or specialist attorneys, and this seems frequently to be the practice.

As other functions, less frequently performed, the generalist lawyer may write the communications on the pension plans to be distributed to employees. He also may have a primary hand in the development of the pension plan itself. The latter function is actually a not infrequent one for union attorneys in the case of multiple-employer plans. Also having developed the plan, the union lawyer may turn out to be its major advisor, along the lines set forth in Chapter V. Finally, both union and management generalist lawyers give advice in connection with collective bargaining.

The specialist attorney is likely to concentrate on the construction of the legal document filed with Internal Revenue and follow through in the negotiations on this, as well as draw up the trust indenture or insurance contract. Apparently the activity of independent specialists in these areas is becoming more common.

The independent specialist attorney will on occasion help develop a pension plan, working with top management as was described in Chapter II. And he will sometimes give advice pertinent to collective bargaining, although he is not likely to appear at the bargaining table.

In general, attorneys in the pension field do not appear to have established themselves as yet to the extent and in the sense that other specialists have, nor in many cases is the field regarded as specialized by the attorneys themselves. There were indications of a considerable amount of "do-it-yourself" work with respect to the preparation of pension documents, a situation which indeed is not all bad, particularly if legalisms are standard and other types of information are more important to the construction of a sound pension document. In some cases also, generalist attorneys, usually in the employ of a client, were said to raise objections to legal work done for the client by specialists in the employ of service or funding agencies of the client. While such objections could very well be for the protection of the client, the intimations were that the objections were on the grounds that specialized knowledge is not required for legal work on private pension plans. This point of view, if it exists, seems not a little dubious in the present and developing legal context of the American private pension movement.[1]

Issues in Accounting for Pensions

Perhaps because the public accountants have gained for themselves a somewhat firmer foothold in the pension field there seems a good deal more discussion of private

---

[1] Cf. Benjamin Aaron, *Legal Status of Employee Benefit Rights under Private Pension Plans* (Homewood, Ill.: Richard D. Irwin, Inc., 1960).

pensions among the accountants. Three issues, significantly all relevant to the matter of pension security, are receiving particular attention among practicing public accountants and in discussions between the public accountants, on the one hand, and their clients and client service agencies, on the other.[2]

The first of these is the question of what is the proper rate of accrual of pension costs for financial accounting purposes. The question has important actuarial aspects, and many public accountants express irritation with the actuarial profession for allegedly not providing a clearer lead. Changes in actuarial assumptions for pension plans on the basis of experience are a focal point for this irritation. The effect on the public accountant is to make him suspicious.

In terms of actual application of cost accrual standards to clients, there appears to be considerable variation among accounting firms. Spirits appear to be rather bold. However, actions are somewhat more circumspect, especially in the important matter of taking exceptions in the accounting certification of the client's annual report. The representative of one large firm of public accountants claimed that through processes of discussion and persuasion employer clients had been persuaded to accept a philosophy of cost accrual which required the funding of 85 to 90 per cent of the estimate by a qualified actuary of the accrued liability of the pension plan, if certification of the client's annual report was to be given without exceptions.[3] The deduction from a 100 per cent standard, he said, was to provide flexibility for tax purposes, given Internal Revenue Service pressures against overfund-

---

[2] For a "source document" see *Accounting Research Bulletins*, No. 47, "Accounting for Costs of Pension Plans," issued by the Committee on Accounting Procedure, American Institute of Accountants, September, 1956. Paragraph 5 is especially relevant.

[3] Such estimates, of course, will vary with the method of determination.

ing. Another public accountant interviewed, however, while he was concerned with the problem of proper cost accrual in light of pension plans, gave no indication that his firm had done anything to emphasize this point with clients.

A second topic of very great interest among accountants appears to be the question of proper treatment of pension fund accretions in the case when capital gains are taken (and presumably fund reductions if capital losses are incurred). This question is, of course, related to the question of proper pension costs. It is important to the public accountant also for its impact on the comparability of successive financial reports. A great capital gain taken, for example, in a period of exceedingly high common stock prices, could be misleading in its connotations of what the employer's future costs of providing pensions might be. The policies of the two firms mentioned above in connection with estimating proper cost accrual, were here, respectively, to require capital gains to be spread over a five-year period for accounting purposes, with capital losses actually incurred through sale of assets being taken immediately, and to require nothing at all.

The third and perhaps most hotly debated question is that concerned with the treatment of actuarial liabilities in financial audits of companies. Many large groups are opposed to treating actuarial liabilities as balance sheet liabilities. There is some justification to this view, given the wording of many if not most private pension plans, which limit the employer's liability to what is in a bank-trusteed pension fund, on deposit with an insurance company, or transferred to a life insuror in the form of purchased benefits.

Many accountants, on the other hand, feel that actuarial liabilities should be treated as balance sheet liabilities. Presumably they are influenced by the likely longevity of existing benefits negotiated under collective bargaining, as well as by a growing number of instances in which the employer in a conventional pension plan has undertaken to guarantee pension benefits.

In a brief review of selected annual reports all certified by the same large public accounting firm, there was, however, no apparent correlation between the treatment by the public accountant of guaranteed and nonguaranteed plans. Whether or not a plan had been negotiated or was conventional also did not seem to make a difference. The one thing which the public accountant appeared to be concerned about was the existence of a substantial unfunded liability. This was noted in his certification of the annual reports which were sampled. Otherwise, however, policies of differential treatment had manifestly not been implemented.

Besides these three matters, two other questions concerning the treatment of pension plan situations by public accountants come up in the literature. One is the inclusion of a statement of the estimated actuarial liability in audit reports of pension funds and plans. This was said not to be the general practice,[4] as the writer himself verified. The criticism is that the typical statement which includes merely a figure on the assets of the plan or fund and another figure on payouts is misleading.

A second additional question involves the appropriateness of methods used in the summary audit by accountants of record keeping and informational flow processes used by employers in connection with their pension plans. In Chapter III this area was noted as a possible administrative gap in the handling of private pension plans and therefore

---

[4] Cf. John A. Williams, CPA, "Actuarial Principles and Pension Plans," *New York Certified Public Accountant*, Vol. XXIX, No. 8 (Aug., 1959), 578–584.

important from the standpoint of pension security. Public accountants appear to be beginning to recognize the existence of this gap and to attempt to do something about it. They apparently, however, feel not quite up to expanding this work as yet. Also there is apparently some resistance from employers. As one writer put it, "The extent of inquiry, review, and discussion as contrasted with a more extensive examination of the aforementioned matters must vary with the responsibility the company has asked the C.P.A. to assume in the audit appointment."[5]

Evaluation

The roles played by attorneys and public accountants quite clearly are pertinent to the objective of pension security in a practical if not always in a theoretical and traditional sense. It is hence quite encouraging to find that the accountants are giving so much thought to such questions as proper costing, disclosure, and valuation. If this thought is followed by intelligent action on a widespread scale there will conceivably be, to the critics of the growth of financial integration of pension plans with the affairs of their sponsoring companies, a satisfactory offset.

Such a role for the accountants must, however, be preceded by careful self-education as to the theory, practice, and financial implications of private pensions, as indeed thoughtful public accountants appear to realize. If this information is not acquired, accounting practice in the pension field is likely to be useful only to accountants.

Practicing attorneys as a group seem as yet not to be as concerned with private pension plans as the public accountant, although, as has been noted, both groups perform

---

[5] Wm. A. Blackman, "Auditing with Actuaries," *Price Waterhouse Review*, Autumn, 1959.

necessary functions. It is to be hoped, however, that this apparent lack of interest will be replaced by an appropriate recognition of those things which turn out to be the special legal problems of the private pension field.

Chapter IX

IMPLICATIONS FOR THE SECURITY
OF PENSION BENEFITS

General Findings

Three problem areas seem to come out of the material presented in the substantive sections of this book. The first of these problems is that there exist apparent administrative "gaps" in the implementation of private pension plans. Noted above were such situations as (1) the asserted inability of outside consultants and internal information sources to communicate fully with each other at early stages of a pension plan; (2) the abandonment or nonexistence of internal audit procedure in the case of single-employer plans; and (3) problems of communication between the actuary and the financial agencies handling pension plans and between the actuary and the public accountant.

The second problem area involves various kinds of possible conflicts of interest. One such situation was noted in connection with the sales development activities of some operators in the funding field. Another came up in connection with the activities of certain pension consultants in dealing with financially weak multiple-employer plans. Still another involves the relationship existing among some pension service agencies and between these and funding agencies. These conflicts appear not to be dominant in the private pension field. Yet they show up from time to time.

A final problem area results from the observation of what appears to be a very definite tendency towards the financial integration, or weaving in, of pension affairs with the total financial affairs of many employers. As has been noted, the manifestations of this financial integration take a number of forms, involving such things as choice of funding agency, annual contribution rates, management of the investment of pension fund assets, and changes in actuarial and investment valuations to go along with the general financial position of the client firms.

The Financial Management Problem

In the case of the first two problem areas the nature of necessary action is obvious. There should be further investigation and there should be necessary remedial action taken by employers, by industries, by professional groups, and if necessary by regulatory bodies. We probably need better auditing, more interchange of information between agencies within and without the sponsoring firm or firms, more frankness in presenting the facts of pension implementation, and perhaps more self-restraint on the part of agencies working in the pension field.

The third problem area is, as has been suggested in the conclusion of Chapter IV, a much more difficult one to deal with, and must be considered very carefully in light of the total circumstances. In a very important sense the financial integration development, with the exceptions noted in Chapter IV, could be a very good thing. Beyond the minimum provided by federal social security legislation pensions in the United States are effectively a responsibility of private enterprise. To the extent that employers sponsoring and contributing to pension plans do not take an active interest in their pension affairs and instead treat the whole business as if it were an unwelcome relative, there must exist in the structure of our private pension system a weakness which can be removed by nothing short of complete assumption of pension responsibilities by a governmental agency. We have in fact instances of this in proposals for changes in the Old Age, Survivors', and Disability Insurance system made by some individuals.

On the other hand, there is cause for concern with the financial integration development, given the evidence that management handles the financing of pensions in light of its own aims; these, it seems clear, are often not entirely consistent with the objective of providing a "sure thing" for pensioners and prospective pensioners. As has been suggested in Chapter IV, pensions for both groups are in many cases looked upon as a part of the employer's total venture strategy. The most crucial aspect of such a policy appears to be in the area of procedures and concepts applicable to the rate of funding.

Our study of the pension agencies indicates that limits to gross financial irresponsibility on the part of pension plan sponsors have been set up by the most important banks, insurance companies, actuaries, consultants, and accountants. These agencies at the same time have generally accorded recognition to the right of pension clients to maneuver financially to some degree.

There was a good deal of evidence to suggest that the limits set were not and could not be "thrown into the faces" of pension clients, so to speak, because of the exigencies of competition for pension business. The more usual agency tactic in the face of unreasonable requests and procedures was to persuade clients into adopting courses of action more consistent with the carrying out of pension responsibilities.

Unfortunately there also was some evidence which

suggested that in a few cases agencies of various kinds could not control their client situations at all and were merely being swept along by the forces of competition and client position. By and large, however, limits seem to exist in the form of agency policies and to stand a fair chance of being enforced.

Some Suggestions for Financial Procedures in Private Pension Implementation

A resolution of the questions posed by the financial integration phenomenon, especially as this involves rate of funding, might be afforded by asking the question of what, if any, support might be afforded the financial efforts of the many responsible employers and pension agencies to maintain adequate and secure private pension plans. The present study has been restricted to the decision and influence processes characteristic of the institutional structure of private pensions. Hence it seems appropriate that any recommendations made here, in this matter of financial aspects, be, as in the case of the reactions given above to administrative integration, linked to the system which has been examined and to the improvement of this system.

We might, in addition, note that implicit in the arrangements which we have in this country for the provision of pensions over and above federal old age insurance are, it would appear, at least three operating social criteria or policies. The first of these is that the administration of pensions is to be decentralized to the level of the business enterprise and/or union and its service agencies. The second is that, consistent with this decentralization, a large area of relatively free decision is to be given to these units. Third, there is to be no prejudice in these arrangements to adequate and secure pensions. Presumably these three criteria reflect such broader policies and objectives of our society as private enterprise, appropriately free competition, and social welfare.

The question thus properly becomes whether or not there is a remedy and support to existing institutional policies against the potential dangers of latitude in funding rate, such that the three criteria discussed above will be satisfied. The writer believes that the answer to this question is in the affirmative and that a pertinent strengthening of the financial system for providing private pensions in the United States is an entirely practical as well as desirable proposition.

Since it is the security of *pensions* that is of interest, it would seem that what ought to be considered first and foremost is some agreement or rule which requires that there be enough money in a pension fund at any time to guarantee the benefits promised to pensioners and to those employees within a few years—possibly five—of retirement. This is something less than a full-scale attack on the matter of funding standards, and to go further might very well be desirable. However, a general stiffening of funding standards involves considerations which are beyond the scope of this book, in view of the demands of our criteria, whereas the present more modest suggestion involves clearly only a minimal ranking of the criteria.

The impact on financially pressed employers of such a minimum requirement as full funding of pensions for the pensioner and near-pensioner group could at times be significant. Yet one wonders whether or not the proper remedy for a financially pressed employer lies elsewhere, possibly in the seeking-out of new intermediate business credit facilities, rather than in the compromising of the pension security of the pensioner and near-pensioner group.

There might well indeed be a temporary exception to this principle of full funding for pensioners and near-pensioners. Presumably, however, such an exception would be appropriate only during the early years of a plan and then only when past service credit is given (whether explicitly reflected in the funding method or not).

The basic proposal and its supplementary aspects just discussed are certainly in a sense ex cathedra from the standpoint of the main direction of the research of this report, which has been concerned with decision and influence processes of private pension plans. On the other hand, the proposals are clearly pointed to by the results of the research and the questions of pension security raised by these results. Whether they are the best proposals which might be made from the standpoint of all the facets of the pension security topic is, of course, a matter which we cannot settle on the basis of the limited view which has been taken of the subject in the present investigation.

Conclusion

The conclusion reached in this study of the decision and influence processes characteristic of American private pension plans is thus that there are some potential and present problem areas, involving administrative, competitive, and financial aspects of our private pension system. The solution of these problems, however, does not seem to call for anything approaching a radical revision of our arrangements and we have assumed this. Consequently what we call for is essentially recognition of the administrative, competitive, and financial practices which seem to be questionable and also of the competing values and objectives implicit in our pension system. With such recognition we can expect and should demand the perfection of our present pension arrangements and the necessary changes which such perfection requires.

Appendix

QUESTIONNAIRE GUIDES USED IN
THE FIELD INVESTIGATION

Client Company Questionnaire

Name of Company (for internal use only)
Contact (for internal use only)

I. Characteristics of plan
    A. Beginning date and circumstances (e.g., negotiated)
    B. Coverage
    C. Funding mechanism(s) if any
    D. IRS status
    E. Benefit formula, contribution system, vesting provisions

II. Division of labor between company and external agencies
    A. Investment of assets
    B. Administration of benefits and records
    C. Actuarial, accounting, and legal
    D. Negotiations

III. Policy and decisions—locus of authority; advisory agencies
    A. Coverage, level of benefits, benefit formula, contribution system
    B. Eligibility (continuity of service), disability, form of payment (lump, etc.), relevant compensation level

119

    C. Investment (if company handles this)

    D. Choice of external agencies (trustee, actuary, accountants, etc.)

    E. Changes since inception of plan

    F. Roles of pension board, treasurer, controller, industrial relations, and top management

IV. Internal co-ordination

    A. Formal committees—composition and subject areas

    B. Information occurrences and requirements among executives and committees

    C. Nature of top-management activity in co-ordination

    D. Impact of collective bargaining, IRS qualification, internal budgeting, and cost control process on internal co-ordination

 V. Co-ordination with external agencies

    A. Extent and nature of contact with banks, actuaries, insurance companies, etc.

    B. Use of supplementary investment advice

    C. Company agent(s) making and receiving contacts (including solicitation)

    D. Processing of external agency recommendations

    E. Reporting requirements of company agents

    F. Problem areas (especially impact of collective bargaining, IRS, budget and cost reduction, investment policy)

VI. Major changes in pension policies, procedures, and implementation—background of these decisions

Questionnaire for Multiple-Employer Plan Trustees

Name of Group (for internal use only)

Contact (for internal use only)

 I. Characteristics of plan

    A. Beginning date and circumstances

    B. Coverage

    C. Funding mechanism

    D. Legal status

    E. Benefit formula, contribution system, vesting provisions

II. Division of labor

    A. With companies and union

    B. With outside agencies

    C. Changes since inception of plan

III. Trustee activities

    A. Frequency and attendance of meetings

    B. Staff work for meetings (if applicable)

    C. Range of decision areas; the most common decision areas

    D. Plan amendments—nature and procedure

IV. Working relationships with companies and union

    A. General character and substance of communications and contacts

    B. Frequency of contact

    C. Persons making contact for employers, union, and trustees

V. Working relationships with external agencies

    A. Frequency and general substance of contacts with lawyers, actuaries, investment counselors, banks, insurance companies, independent administrators, accountants, etc.

    B. Persons making contacts (both ends)

    C. Processing of recommendations from external agencies

    D. Problem areas

VI. Major changes in policies, procedures, and implementation since inception—character and background of these changes, if any

Questionnaire for Funding Agencies

> Name of Company (for internal use only)
> Contact (for internal use only)

I. Functions performed in case of pension plans
   A. Range of functions
   B. Most common functions
   C. Allocation of responsibilities within your organization
II. Working relationships with client
   A. General character and substance of communications and contacts
   B. Frequency of contact with regard to the several functions
   C. Persons involved in contacts (both ends)
III. Working relationships with other agencies on individual pension plans
   A. Client actuaries, administrators, accountants, investment counselors, etc.
   B. Regulatory agencies
IV. Major policies and procedures necessary for handling pension activities—character and explanation (where applicable)
   A. Clients' suggestions on investment
   B. Costing (administration, actuarial—charges to fund)
   C. Compliance (of client) with regulatory agencies
   D. Segregation of accounts—contributory and noncontributory plans
   E. Large and small plans
   F. Multiple and single employers
   G. Split funding and multiple trustees

V. Changes in working relationships and policies—character and explanation

Questionnaire for Investment Counselors, Independent Administrators, Actuaries, Accountants, Lawyers, and Insurance Brokers

Name of Agency (for internal use only)
Contact (for internal use only)

I. Functions performed in case of pension plans
   A. Range of functions
   B. Most common functions
   C. Allocation of responsibilities within your organization
II. Working relationships with client
   A. General character and substance of communications and contacts
   B. Frequency of contact with regard to the several functions
   C. Persons involved in contacts (both ends)
III. Working relationships with other agencies on individual pension plans
   A. Client bank and/or insurance company
   B. Other client service agencies
   C. Regulatory agencies
IV. Major policies and procedures necessary for handling pension activities—character and explanation
   A. Clients' suggestions concerning performance of your function(s)
   B. Charges to client for performance of functions
   C. Compliance (of client) with regulatory agencies

D. Record keeping, analysis, and communication for client (where applicable)

E. Large and small plans

F. Multiple and single employers

G. Split funding and multiple trustees

V. Changes in working relationships and policies—character and explanation

INDEX

125

This book has been set on the Linotype in 12
and 10 point Bodoni Book, leaded 2 points.
Chapter numbers and titles are in 14 point
Bodoni Bold #275. The size of the type page
is 24 by 40½ picas.